Strangers on Our
Strangers in C

Inter-Disciplinary Press

Publishing Advisory Board

Inter-Disciplinary Press is a part of *Inter-Disciplinary.Net*
A Global Network for Dynamic Research and Publishing

2016

Strangers on Our Doorstep and Strangers in Our House:

Inter-Disciplinary Approaches to Fears and Anxieties

Edited by

Magdalena Hodalska, Catalin Ghita and Izabela Dixon

Inter-Disciplinary Press

Oxford, United Kingdom

The *Inter-Disciplinary Press* is part of *Inter-Disciplinary.Net* – a global network for research and publishing. The *Inter-Disciplinary Press* aims to promote and encourage the kind of work which is collaborative, innovative, imaginative, and which provides an exemplar for inter-disciplinary and multi-disciplinary publishing.

British Library Cataloguing in Publication Data. A catalogue record for this book is available from the British Library.

Inter-Disciplinary Press, Priory House, 149B Wroslyn Road, Freeland, Oxfordshire. OX29 8HR, United Kingdom.
+44 (0)1993 882087

ISBN: 978-1-84888-443-4
First published in the United Kingdom in Paperback format in 2016. First Edition.

Table of Contents

Introduction:
Fear of Strangers in Our Minds

Magdalena Hodalska, Catalin Ghita and Izabela Dixon

As pointed out by the French historian Jean Delumeau and recalled by Alina Cherata in the first chapter of this volume, for centuries people have harboured fears of alterity and the unknown:

> People with dogs' heads who oinked and barked; headless men, with eyes on their bellies; people who sheltered themselves from the sun by lying on their backs and raising their only leg to shade their faces – these are depictions of Indians that circulated in Western Europe in the Middle Ages. It was a fantasy world created to induce fear, as sailors from various countries tried to impress and discourage their competitors by spreading terrifying tales about their journeys to remote places.[1]

To audiences susceptible to fear such accounts were disquieting despite the fact that the seemingly terrifying Others lived too far away to be of any threat. It is evident, however, that these images captured people's imagination. This may be because far too often Strangers, Foreigners, Outlanders, Migrants or Invaders have wreaked havoc in people's territories and minds. And the general feeling today is that they continue to do so.

At first glance, there is virtually no resemblance 'between the fear-ridden, bigoted world of mediaeval Europe, built mostly around local communities, and today's open society, in which intercultural communication and the ideal of transcending spatial and mental borders are centre-stage.'[2] However, we may be experiencing a revival of old phobias and the onset of new fears not only rooted in imaginary phenomena, but also stimulated by actual events.

Strangers on Our Doorstep and Strangers in Our House: Inter-Disciplinary Approaches to Fears and Anxieties is one of the outcomes of a broadly-encompassing project initiated by Magdalena Hodalska and Catalin Ghita with the support of Inter-Disciplinary.Net. This dialogic and inter-disciplinary volume seeks to explore fears and anxieties not only with scientific detachment, but also with empathy.

When on the 29th of July 2014 we met at Mansfield College, Oxford, Great Britain, to discuss *Fears and Anxieties in the 21st Century: The European Context* at the first edition of this Global Conference, the conference coincided with several events and their aftermaths. It was shortly after a Malaysian Airlines passenger plane was shot down over Ukraine, as well as the time of the military occupation of Crimea, during which many Ukrainians sought refuge in the European Union as

numerous EU politicians blamed East-European immigrants for the problems
certain member States were facing.

As will become apparent, contemporary fears and anxieties take on different
hues and guises. They may be clothed in green military jackets or in the rags of
those who dared to cross the borders of their countries in an attempt to escape to a
better world. These fears, and many others, are recorded on the pages of this
volume.

The thematic principle around which the chapters of this volume revolve may
be expressed by the ancient binomial *extra muros/intra muros*. In other words, the
authors have focused on the fears aroused by events beyond the confines of one's
House, be that taken literally or metaphorically, as well as within its confines. But
let us now get to the point.

The first part of the book, *Fear of Foreigners and Neighbours*, examines the
various fears and anxieties of people living in both the Western and the
Central/Eastern part of the continent of Europe, namely in the European Union and
in the Post-Soviet Bloc.

Stefania Alina Cherata's analysis of the fear of alterity in contemporary
Europe, is illustrated by the phenomenon of migration within the EU, with
immigrants portrayed by local politicians and the media as 'the evil enemy' and a
threat to the security and social well-being of local residents. Cherata discusses the
rise of nationalism and anti-immigrant sentiment in certain areas of Europe and
argues that the century-old fear of alterity may still be at the core of the
contemporary European mentality, regardless of the declared adherence to a
common European identity and the professed openness and sensitivity towards
other cultures, which remain the key values promoted by European institutions in
the context of a globalized world.

Yet perhaps the reality is somewhat different, not only in the West, but also in
the East. The problems which are illustrated by Agnieszka Konopelko and
Katarzyna Czerewacz-Filipowicz in their studies of political tensions and
economic strains in the Post-Soviet Area, with the former analysing the case of
Transnistria, and the latter exploring the Fears of Neighbours nurtured by the
citizens of countries founded after the collapse of the Soviet regime, are
exacerbated by old enmities, while at the same time alleviated according to
economic needs necessitating certain levels of cooperation.

Fear of Foreigners and Neighbours is in fact the *Fear Strangers on Our
Doorstep*. Fear may also be cultivated in literature and poetry, as is illustrated by
Catalin Ghita in his in-depth study of patriotic poems. Narratives are a mirror
reflecting contemporary anxieties. Narratives about the Haunted House allow Clara
Pallejá-López to introduce the concept of gender-conditioned construction of
meaning. Her study opens the second part of the book, which discusses *Fears of
Strangers in Our House*. Strangers found *intra muros* can be more threatening to
what is perceived as 'our' spirit than those coming from the outside. And this is

crucial for the studies presented in this section. Writing about fictional Haunted Houses, Pallejá-López shows convincingly how fear responses can be transmitted from one generation to another and, moreover, how these can be conditioned by gender.

Tensions between men and women living in the same House are discussed in detail by Izabela Dixon and Magdalena Hodalska. The two authors examine the communication of Emotional Strangers occupying the same physical space, who were once in love, but now are perhaps tied only by common financial commitments or a child, and who exhibit a considerable degree of mutual antipathy. Providing factual accounts of authentic situations, the chapter 'Commitment to Self' gives an insight into a Real-Life Haunted House of the 21st Century, where men and women live as total strangers.

Emotions revolving around relationships and family members may influence a significant number of fears and anxieties, a fact which is illustrated by a cross-cultural study focusing on both Indonesia and Germany. Shally Novita and Evelin Witruk show how anxiety related to dyslexia is conditioned by culture and family and that this contributes significantly to the level of stress experienced in life. In the final pages of the book, Sukran Karatas gives scientific, physical and metaphysical explanations of Fears and Anxieties in relation to spiritual life and well-being.

The main theme of the book – humanity's constant fears and anxieties – is so complex and multifaceted that it requires several minds to identify it effectively and subsequently to place it in a relevant context. The task of the editors has, therefore, been to ensure the structural polyphony of the chapters and at the same time preserve the specificity of the various auctorial voices. *Unitas in pluralitate* would seem to be the working motto of this ambitious collection of essays, which unites disciplines, such as history, psychology, political science, linguistics, literature and theology.

The layperson might justifiably ask him or herself: why should one devote so much space and energy to a topic that even children understand in un unmediated manner? Let us answer this in an oblique fashion by calling the reader's attention to a significant literary context. In one of his numerous letters to Milena Jesenská, Franz Kafka emphasized that fear lay at the core of his being: 'Indeed, it is my substance and probably the best part of me.'[3]

Whereas none of the authors of the present book's chapters would venture to claim a level of sensitivity comparable to that of Kafka, they can all safely assert, together with the editors, that fear is one of the most pervasive social emotions, which, alongside anxiety and phobias, helps to configure the collective imagery of today's convoluted world. In the absence of fear, life would be inconceivable, for fear may bring out courage, dignity and responsibility. It is only in the face of fear and danger that one can define the measure of one's true being.

Notes

[1] Stefania Alina Cherata, 'Invasions and Tidal Waves: Fictionalizing EU Migration', in this volume.
[2] Ibid.
[3] Franz Kafka, *Letters to Milena*, trans. Philip Boehm (New York: Schocken Books, 1990).

Bibliography

Kafka, Franz. Letters to Milena. Translated by Philip Boehn. New York: Schocken Books, 1990.

Magdalena Hodalska, PhD, was a freelance reporter and is now a Senior Lecturer in the Institute of Journalism, Media and Social Communication at the Jagiellonian University in Kraków, Poland. Her research interests are media narratives, discourse and language, war correspondence and fear in the media.

Catalin Ghita, PhD, Dr Habil, was a Japanese Government Scholar at Tohoku University and is now Professor of Comparative Literature and Cultural Studies at the University of Craiova, Romania. His research interests are: fear in literature, visionary poetry, romanticism and cultural exchanges between Europe and Asia.

Izabela Dixon, PhD, specialises in cognitive linguistics, metaphor and the study of contemporary fears and anxieties. She has published numerous articles on a wide range of subjects including conceptual metaphors of fear and evil, cognitive definitions of monsters, ethno-linguistics, US and THEM schema and aspects of the 'war on terror' discourse.

Part I

Fear of Foreigners and Neighbours

Invasions and Tidal Waves: Fictionalizing EU Migration

Stefania Alina Cherata

Abstract
Fear of alterity has accompanied the development of human societies from the earliest times. Its forms, however, have changed over the years, from overt rejection and sometimes physical aggression against outsiders to more subtle patterns of scepticism concealed behind the professed allegiance to cosmopolitanism and intercultural dialogue. Today's Europe sports an intriguing interplay of contradictory tendencies. On the one hand, European institutions officially promote the ideal of transcending physical and mental frontiers and creating a common European identity intended to replace the more traditional-and limiting-national cultures. On the other hand, we are witnessing a revival of fear, nationalism and xenophobia, prompted by the very necessity of adapting to life within a European community. The present chapter aims to show how this intricate combination of openness and fear-based rejection of alterity manifests itself in the context of EU migration. More precisely, I will examine the way in which, despite officially displayed foreigner-friendly attitudes, local politicians and the media often augment fears of 'the fiendish other' by portraying migration as a threat to public security and blaming immigrants for various social and political problems. Linguistically, this securitizing approach to migration is constructed through an extensive use of metaphor and hyperbole, which increases dimensions and confers symbolical significance to the people and events involved. The result is an accentuated sense of fear and a feeling that immigrants are 'the evil enemy', waiting to 'invade' their country of destination. I will illustrate these points by drawing on a case study: the alleged murder of Italian citizen Giovanna Reggiani by a Romanian of Roma origin, Romulus Mailat, in 2007, a few months after Romania's European integration.

Key Words: Fear of alterity, EU, immigration, fiction, securitization, Romania, Roma minority, criminality.

*****

1. Fear of Alterity: An Introduction

People with dogs' heads who oinked and barked; headless men, with eyes on their bellies; people who sheltered themselves from the sun by lying on their backs and raising their only leg to shade their faces - these are depictions of Indians that circulated in Western Europe in the Middle Ages. It was a fantasy world created to induce fear, as sailors from various countries tried to impress and discourage their competitors by spreading terrifying tales about their journeys to remote places. The fact that such stories were deemed plausible relies on two apparently contradictory reasons: Europeans' fear of alterity and the unknown, doubled by their fascination with far-off realms.[1]

Fear of the other was omnipresent in Western Europe throughout the Middle Ages. In many cases, it was accompanied by parochial mentalities and a general sense of hostility towards people coming from other places. In the countryside, the locals organized *chivaris*, grotesque performances during which they hit pots and pans, whistled and booed to show their disapproval whenever one of the village girls married someone who was not part of the community. There were also frequent fights between the inhabitants of neighbouring villages. Moreover, if an outsider was beaten by a local, when confronted with the authorities, people manifested their solidarity with the perpetrator. Another phenomenon which is symptomatic of mediaeval Europeans' fear and rejection of alterity was the tendency to blame the spreading of epidemics on the Jews. Not least, during the 15th and 16th centuries, the practice of portraying other nations in pejorative terms was quite common among West Europeans. In fact, there were xenophobic movements until much later, in the 18th century.[2]

At first sight, there seems to be no resemblance between the fear-ridden, bigoted world of mediaeval Europe, built mostly around local communities, and today's open society, in which intercultural communication and the ideal of transcending spatial and mental borders are centre-stage. Adherence to a European identity, as opposed to the local or national identities of previous centuries, as well as openness and sensitivity towards other cultures are some of the key values promoted by European institutions in the context of a globalized world. Yet despite these significant transformations, there are signals which suggest that the century-old fear of alterity may still be at the core of contemporary European mentalities.

One such indicator is the outcome of the 2014 European elections, when far-right parties topped the polls in countries like France, Britain, Hungary, Austria or Denmark. International media spoke of a 'sweep'.[3] an 'earthquake',[4] or, in some cases, of a 'march on Brussels'[5] of the extreme right. This alarmist phrasing overlooked the differences between the various far-right parties and the national contexts that led to their success. It also failed to take into account the good results obtained by left-wing parties in some European states (Spain, Portugal, Greece, Romania) and the decline of far-right formations which had previously held seats in the European Parliament.[6]

Such nuances notwithstanding, the victories of far-right parties like the French National Front (24.85%), the Austrian Freedom Party (19.7%), the Danish People's Party (26.6%) or Britain's UKIP (26.6%) point to a rise in nationalism and anti-immigrant sentiment in some areas of Europe. This becomes clear if we consider the openly anti-foreigner messages these parties sent out during the electoral campaign. France's Marine Le Pen called immigration 'a mortal threat to civil peace in France',[7] while Austrian leader Heinz-Christian Strache emphasized his opposition to Muslim immigration, though he claimed he was not animated by xenophobia because he 'ate kebabs'. The founder of the Danish People's Party, Pia Kjærsgaard, also championed nationalistic views. On one occasion, she responded to Swedish criticism by saying: 'If they want to turn Stockholm, Gothenburg or Malmö into a Scandinavian Beirut, with clan wars, honour killings and gang rapes, let them do it. We can always put a barrier on the Øresund Bridge'.[8] In Britain, one UKIP election poster showed a builder begging for money. The picture was accompanied by the words: 'EU policy at work. British workers are hit hard by unlimited cheap labour'. Another poster displayed a giant hand pointing at the viewer, along with the question: '26 million people in Europe are looking for work. And whose jobs are they after?'[9] There were also other right-wing parties that won seats in the European Parliament, though their percentages were lower. Among them were the Dutch far-right Party for Freedom (13.2%), which campaigned against Muslim immigration and 'Islamification', and the Hungarian Neo-Nazi party Jobbik (14.7%), whose representatives suggested that the country's Jewish inhabitants should sign a special register. Other Neo-Nazi parties that won seats in the European Parliament were Greece's Golden Dawn (9.4%) and Germany's NPD (admittedly only 1%).[10]

The discrepancy between the official advocacy of foreigner-friendly attitudes and political correctness on the one hand and the public support granted in individual states to parties with an overt anti-foreigner and anti-immigrant discourse on the other indicates that xenophobia and fear of alterity are not extinct in today's Europe, but take on more complex and sophisticated forms compared to the past. This tendency is particularly noticeable in the context of EU migration, a circumstance which challenges the members of national communities to accept and integrate foreigners. It is this type of direct everyday contact with the other that provides the acid test for alluring concepts like European unity and intercultural communication.

The present chapter explores fear of alterity in contemporary Europe, as illustrated by the phenomenon of EU migration. It starts by showing that, to a large extent, the fear and scepticism towards foreigners manifested in some European states at the moment can be described as corollaries of the attempt to create a transnational European identity (§2). Subsequently, it focuses on fear of alterity in the more specific context of European migration and argues that one of its consequences is a tendency to fictionalize reality (§3). Finally, a case study is presented to illustrate the details of this fictionalization process (§4).

2. Fear as a By-Product of Creating a European Identity

According to French anthropologist Claude Lévi-Strauss, the tendency to reject people and customs that clash with our familiar environment and our view of the world is a deeply ingrained trait of the human species. It goes back a long way and continues to lurk below the surface of civilized behaviour, ready to be redeemed whenever the norms and values of civilization slip away.[11] To some extent, such a revival appears to be taking place in today's Europe, where the lofty values supported by European institutions are sometimes substituted in practice by the combination of fear and rejection of the other. But what exactly is causing this displacement?

Before the era of globalization, the most popular forms of social and political organization were local communities and nation states, both of them characterized by a relatively clear mental and physical delimitation of autochthonous identity against outside influences. Nation states in this traditional sense possessed territorial sovereignty, bound up with a sense of cultural homogeneity and a collective social identity. Beck has described this view as a 'container model' of culture.[12] Container cultures comprise a number of container-like sub-systems (e.g. social classes and ethnic groups); moreover, they have a national economy, literature, history etc., which can be described in isolation.[13] The unity of these cultures is artificial, however, as it abstracts from both internal distinctions and external influences.[14] In this sense, nation states may be regarded as bounded fictions: 'A people [...] is [...] a question of myths and forms. It requires a legend and a map. Ancestors and enemies. A people is a population plus contours and story-tellers'.[15]

As a result of globalization, the clear-cut distinctions between national cultures have been challenged. The European Union was founded chiefly for economic and political reasons. This pragmatic purpose was nevertheless closely related to the idea of transcending national borders and the limitations of container cultures. Yet although the concept was appealing, the practice of a united Europe soon proved to be fraught with difficulties for at least two reasons:

> Globalization may have eroded the powers of nation states as sovereign political entities, but the national principle and national identity remain central to the conferral of political legitimacy in most modern democracies.[16]

At the same time, the very elements that unite members of national communities (e.g. language, history or religion) are the ones undermining the creation of a transnational European identity. These concrete aspects of life within a community are more likely to support a sense of common identity than the rather abstract values promoted by European institutions. For this reason, despite widespread talks of an emerging European identity, it is still easier to rally around the shared ingredients of national cultures.[17]

The context of a united Europe has led to a more frequent and intense interaction between the representatives of various cultures and, consequently, to a need for adjustment. Theoretically, this should have resulted in greater openness and fewer constraints through mental and physical borders. In practice, nevertheless, a surprising phenomenon occurred. When faced with the necessity of living and communicating with people of other nationalities, a large number of Europeans began to fear losing their autonomy and cultural identity, as well as their social and economic well-being. This brought about a relapse into the archaic fear of alterity and, as a self-defence mechanism, a return to nationalism:

> Paradoxically, European integration has provoked a renaissance of ethnicity and nationalism-particularly of the regional kind- much of it mixed up with fears about loss of sovereignty and identity and the promise of wealth and status in a future 'Europe of the Regions'.[18]

This development exemplifies a tendency described by French philosopher and journalist Régis Debray in his essay *Éloge des frontières*. Debray argues that the enthusiastic desire to eliminate borders, which is so characteristic of today's globalized society, is in fact unnatural and unrealistic. The attempt to abolish frontiers will inevitably generate new demarcation lines, writes the French author,[19] and, in a sense, this is precisely what has been happening in Europe in recent years. By attempting to supersede nationalism and xenophobia, the EU has ironically ended up reinforcing them, so that, in opposition to the ideal of a united Europe, fear of alterity has found its way back into contemporary European societies. This apparently contradictory evolution is most clearly epitomized by migration.

3. EU Migration: Creating a Political Fiction

In terms of migration, the European Union seems to be confronted with a paradox. On the one hand, immigrants are necessary, as they provide convenient workforce and compensate for the demographic lows that characterize a large number of European states at present.[20] On the other hand, in most European countries, the dwindling prosperity in the wake of the financial crisis has given rise to a sense of social insecurity, while also placing increased pressure on national social welfare systems. In this context, there has been a tendency to reject migration due to locals' fear of losing their welfare benefits to foreigners. Immigrants were considered illegitimate recipients of social assistance in communities they did not belong to, an attitude that Huysmans describes as 'welfare chauvinism'.[21] Scepticism towards immigrants was further enhanced by fears over losing national tradition, cultural identity and societal homogeneity.[22]

Anxieties of this kind were skilfully manipulated and capitalized on by politicians, who in many cases amplified them and encouraged basic nationalistic reactions:

> The political response to this situation has been a populist, cheap and risky one: *we'll take care of you!* France to the French, Italy

to the Italians and so on .... Parties/governments have thus fallen
into their own trap, caught between the political commitment to
limit and control migration and the socio-economic necessity of
stimulating it. In most cases, this resulted in half-baked,
incoherent, interpretable laws, which in political terms stated
something that was at odds with their economic purpose, which
set sentinels at the front door of migration, but left the back door
open, and which not only failed to deal with mobility in a
rational way but (often consciously) let it go out of hand even
more, promoting in fact illegal migration and black-market
work.[23]

The outcome was a public validation of fear and social insecurity. Immigrants
became scapegoats for the social and economic problems of the day, a role that
seemed plausible in the eyes of the local population on account of their outsider
status. In a large number of countries, migration was subject to securitization
approaches: it was officially presented as a major threat to national identity and
security, requiring exceptional emergency measures.[24]
Originally, this applied to migration from outside the European Union. While
EU-internal frontiers were being lifted, control at the external borders was being
reinforced. In this way, an association between migration and national security was
created:

To make the issues of border control a security question [...], the
internal market had to be connected to an internal security
problematique. A key element in this process was the
identification of a particular side-effect of the creation of the
internal market. One expected that the market would not only
improve free movement of law-abiding agents, but would also
facilitate illegal and criminal activities by terrorists, international
criminal organizations, asylum-seekers and immigrants. The
institutionalization of police and customs co-operation, and the
discourses articulating this particular side-effect, produced a
security continuum connecting border control, terrorism,
international crime and migration.[25]

The idea that migration might endanger national security was extrapolated to a
new context when central and eastern European countries joined the EU in 2004
and 2007. Migrants from inside the EU were now presented as a serious threat to
the security of their host countries.[26]

Terms such as *invasion* or *flood* were often used by politicians and the media to refer to immigrants, in an effort to magnify the impact on public consciousness and account for exceptional security measures:

> Advocates of securitized migration were keen on using the symbolic power of the metaphor of invasion, presenting images of tidal waves of refugee movements, alarmist perceptions that Western countries were being flooded with migrants, and views of looming large-scale immigration as imminent threats to national security.[27]

This apocalyptic rhetoric engendered a *Hannibal ante portas* effect, a political fiction intended to instil fear in the majority population, who was given the impression that it was under siege and had to face an external enemy.[28]

The next chapter shows how such a securitizing fiction of migration was constructed during one of the most widely publicized events involving Romanian immigrants in the EU: the murder of Giovanna Reggiani in October 2007.

4. The Reggiani Case

In the wake of Romania's EU entry, a series of crimes committed by Romanian nationals were reported in the Italian press. In spring 2007, a Romanian prostitute killed an Italian woman by thrusting an umbrella into her eye, and then another Romanian murdered an old Italian couple with axe blows. In summer of the same year, film director Giuseppe Tornatore was assaulted by three Romanians. Finally, in October, a Romanian man raped a 40-year-old Italian woman on the steps of a church.[29]

In 2007, 50% of the foreign criminals in Italy were reported to be of Romanian, Moroccan and Albanian origin. 37% of the total number of thefts and 15% of the murders in Italy were attributed to Romanians.[30] It was against this backdrop that Giovanna Reggiani's murder occurred.

A. The Events

On 30 October 2007, Giovanna Reggiani, the 47-year-old wife of a naval captain, went shopping in central Rome. On her way home, on a road that led away from the Tor di Quinto train station, she fell into the hands of an attacker. After being robbed and beaten, she was eventually left lying in a ditch. She was found in a coma and taken to a hospital, where she died two days after the assault.

The man accused of murdering her was Nicolae Romulus Mailat, a Romanian of Roma origin who lived in the gypsy camp at Tor di Quinto. He was incriminated by Emilia Neamtu, another camp inhabitant, who claimed to have seen him commit the murder and drag the body of the fainted victim under a bridge. Giovanna Reggiani's handbag was found under Mailat's bed.[31]

B. The Trial

However, Mailat denied having beaten or killed Giovanna Reggiani. He only admitted to stealing her handbag, and claimed he had been accompanied by another man, the son of the self-declared witness, Gheorghe Neamtu, whom he accused of being the real murderer.

In a 2009 article, journalist Guglielmo Ragozzino made a detailed analysis of Mailat's trial. He argued that the two witnesses whose statements led to Mailat's conviction were not present at the trial and their versions of the events were unreliable and partially incompatible. Ragozzino pointed out that the main witness, Emilia Neamtu, couldn't even remember all her children; as far as Giovanna Reggiani's aggression was concerned, she seemed confused and made a number of contradictory statements.[32]

The second witness was Dorin Obedea, the father of Mailat's girlfriend. He was in possession of Giovanna Reggiani's mobile phone, which he declared he had received from Mailat when the latter had been arrested (a fact denied by the superintendent in charge of the arrest). He claimed that he had witnessed the aggression from a hiding place, and that Mailat had handed him Giovanna Reggiani's handbag containing a large amount of money (another allegation which proved to be false). Like Mailat, he mentioned a third person, Gheorghe Neamtu, who, he claimed, had come with his mother, Emilia. The latter, however, made no mention of her son when questioned.[33]

Despite shaky evidence and doubtful witnesses, Mailat was sentenced first to twenty-nine years in prison, and eventually received a life sentence. He considered himself a scapegoat for the crimes committed by Romanian communitary citizens in Italy:

> I have no words, I surrender to divine justice. I didn't want to say anything during the trial because I understood it would be pointless. They want someone to blame for such a serious offence and I think I was unlucky enough to be the scapegoat.[34]

C. Political Reactions

The day after the attack on Giovanna Reggiani, Romano Prodi's centre-left cabinet met in an emergency session and issued a decree which allowed prefects-the local representatives of the interior ministry-to expel the citizens of other EU states without a trial if they were considered a threat to public security. The decree was strongly criticized by the European Parliament, NGOs, the Italian League for Human Rights and the European Roma Grassroots organization as being at odds with the 2004/38/CE directive, according to which EU citizens are free to travel and live on the territory of other member states.[35]

Interior Minister Giuliano Amato explained that the decree aimed to 'prevent the terrible tiger of xenophobia, the racist beast, from breaking out of the cage'.[36]

Carlo Mosca, the Prefect of Rome, argued that utmost severity was the only appropriate response to 'beasts,' and that 'infested fish' ought to be removed in order to protect honest citizens, including those coming from other countries.[37] Rome's mayor, Walter Veltroni, made sweeping assertions about an entire category of people:

> From June until today there have been a number of violent episodes that point to a change of climate [...]. Unfortunately, all these episodes go back to the same matrix... in this, as in other big cities, there has been a massive flow of communitary citizens, not extracommunitary, not immigrants who come here to live, but a category characterized by criminality.[38]

He called for immediate action: 'Before Romania's entry into the EU Rome was the safest of cities. [...] We need to start over with repatriations'.[39] There were indeed police raids on several Roma camps. Barracks were pulled down, and immigrants without appropriate papers were arrested.

On the other side of the political spectrum, Silvio Berlusconi blamed Romano Prodi and his government for the situation, and suggested a ban on Romanian workers.[40] In an interview to the *Corriere della Sera,* Gianfranco Fini, leader of the right-wing National Alliance and one of Berlusconi's key allies, launched a harsh attack on the Roma. He claimed they 'have no scruples about kidnapping children or using their own children for begging', 'consider theft to be virtually legitimate and not immoral', and feel that it is 'up to the women to work, even through prostitution'. He concluded that 'to talk of integration with people with a "culture" of that sort is pointless.'[41] The public outcry contributed to Berlusconi's return to power in April 2008, and to the election of rightwing Gianni Alemanno as mayor of Rome. As part of his 'Pact for Rome', Alemanno promised the removal of 20,000 immigrants and the destruction of immigrant camps around the city.[42]

Romanian Prime Minister Calin Popescu Tariceanu expressed his regret and willingness to cooperate in finding a solution to the 'Italian issue'. Romanian police were sent to Rome in an attempt to set up a joint police force. At the same time, Tariceanu asked his Italian counterpart Romano Prodi to ensure the protection of Romanian citizens in Italy against xenophobic acts. The two Prime Ministers also discussed the difficulties of integrating the Roma.[43] President Traian Basescu stated that most problems related to Romanian immigrants were caused by Roma ethnics and that their integration required a joint European strategy.[44] He also expressed concern that the measures adopted by the Italian government might be directed against Romanians in general rather than against Romanian criminals alone. A very controversial attitude was that of the Romanian Minister of Foreign Affairs, Adrian Cioroianu, who declared he was considering buying a piece of land in the Egyptian desert and exiling all those who stained Romania's image there. He was accused of fostering far-right attitudes and forced to step down.[45]

D. Press Coverage

In the first hours after the attack on Giovanna Reggiani, it was believed that the victim was a woman belonging to the Roma community. The news was, therefore, confined to a small box in a couple of newspapers. However, as soon as the real nationality of the victim had transpired, the story made the headlines of all the major Italian newspapers.[46] The nationalities of those involved were indeed paramount to the way in which the Italian media reported the Reggiani case. Grazia Naletto points out that Mailat's Romanian nationality was mentioned in most articles, usually starting from the headlines.[47]

A high level of symbolism was also apparent in the way in which the Romanian press approached the Reggiani case. Ionut Codreanu and Nicoleta Fotiade analysed 78 articles published between 1 and 10 November 2007 in the three most popular Romanian newspapers of the time (*Jurnalul National, Evenimentul Zilei* and the tabloid *Libertatea*). They remarked that in a large number of articles the attributes used to describe Roma ethnics were pejorative, and Mailat was given no benefit of the doubt.[48] There was also a tendency to exaggerate and overgeneralize in order to trigger a strong emotional response.[49] The authors concluded that both Romanian and Italian journalists had turned 'a crime into a criminal phenomenon, a communitary citizen into an immigrant, an individual into an ethnic group and an ethnic group into a nation.'[50]

E. Social Response

The Italian public reacted strongly to the murder of Giovanna Reggiani, partly due to the inflammatory rhetoric used by politicians and the media. A number of participants in the funeral shouted: 'We're afraid!', 'Make laws!', 'Romanians, out of the country!'.[51] A group of ten Italians armed with knives, metal bars and chains attacked four Romanian citizens in a parking lot in Rome. Three days later, in Monterotondo, an incendiary bottle was thrown against the window of a shop administered by a Romanian. On the same day, in Rome, a man insulted and spat on a Romanian woman on the bus, provoking no reaction from the other passengers.[52] On 4 November 2007, several hundred Italians demonstrated in Rome, urging Romanian immigrants to leave the country. In a survey published by *Corriere della Sera*, 70% of Italian respondents declared that peaceful co-existence with the Roma was impossible.[53]

F. Discussion

The Reggiani case illustrates, in a nutshell, some of the major challenges facing the European Union today: the difficulties connected with forging a supranational European identity; the fear of losing one's national identity and well-being to outsiders and the consequent reinforcement of nationalism and xenophobia; the shift from national to European problems (e.g. Roma integration).

Giovanna Reggiani's murder and the reactions it spurred showed that the ideal of a common European identity was still far from becoming a reality. From the onset, the nationalities of those involved were brought into the foreground by the media, and the crime rapidly acquired a symbolic dimension. From an unfortunate event it became a confrontation between Italians and Romanians. The symbolism was reinforced by an alarmingly high number of discriminatory political statements and by the controversial decree adopted by the Prodi cabinet. The fears of the Italian public were thus confirmed and fostered, resulting in a series of xenophobic manifestations in the days and months following the murder.

The Romanian press also attached a symbolic quality to the crime, promoting fear of xenophobic acts and a sense of rebellion against the Roma. Some politicians followed suit, and singled out the Roma minority as the main reason for the negative image of Romanians abroad. This struck a sensitive chord with the Romanian public, due to the difficulties of Roma integration and the frequent confusion between Roma and Romanians at an international level.

The role played by the Roma minority in the Reggiani case drew attention to the fact that Roma integration, originally regarded as a Romanian issue, had acquired European relevance with the country's EU entry. As President Basescu stated at the time, it had become necessary to find a solution at a European level. The attitude of the Italian government, however, showed an unwillingness to take joint responsibility for Roma integration. Italy chose instead to repatriate the citizens who might create problems. A similar response came from the French authorities in 2010, when hundreds of Roma were sent back to Romania, contrary to European values and legislation.

Another interesting phenomenon exemplified by the Reggiani case was the avoidance of responsibility. Italian officials blamed immigrants (and, in some cases, specifically Romanians) for the crime, while right-wing politicians held the Italian government accountable, and simultaneously reinforced the public's fear of immigrants. Romanians in turn tended to blame Giovanna Reggiani's murder and the Romanian-Italian crisis on the Roma.

A culprit was needed, and amid mounting fears and the high symbolism attached to the case, Romulus Mailat was convicted to life in prison despite inconclusive evidence. The Italian public did not doubt the fairness of the sentence because Mailat was Romanian and a pattern of Romanian criminality had already been established in Italian consciousness. Romanians did not doubt it because he was of Roma origin, and there was an equally strong association between Roma and criminality in the mind of the Romanian public.

As statistics showed, Romanian criminality in Italy was indeed relatively high. In the same way, the problematic integration of the Roma community also had a realistic foundation. It was the absolutization of these aspects and the indiscriminate conflation of a person with an entire nation or ethnic group that created an atmosphere of fear and hatred and may have been responsible for an unfair prison sentence.

5. Conclusions

The ideal of a united Europe provides a strong counterpoise to the nation-centred world of previous centuries. By trying to abolish the strict physical and mental boundaries between countries and cultures, it also seems to put an end to related negative phenomena like fear of alterity, nationalism and xenophobia. Yet although contact between people of different nationalities is more extensive today than ever before, a closer look will reveal that, far from being eradicated, fear of the other is still very much at the heart of contemporary European societies. The forms it assumes, however, are more elaborate and veiled than they were in the past.

Despite official attempts to replace national cultures with a unifying continental identity, Europeans continue to feel a strong commitment to their national communities, to which they are bound by a common history, language, religion, shared customs etc. At the same time, the interaction with members of other nationalities often generates fears of losing welfare benefits and cultural identity. In many cases, the response is an ironic return to nationalism and xenophobia.

This tendency is clearly illustrated by recent developments in EU migration. Due to an enhanced sense of social and economic insecurity after the 2008 financial crisis, Europeans have started to fear for their safety and well-being. Against this background, immigrants are often perceived as a threat to national security, identity and prosperity. The inclination to reject outsiders as a menace, an attitude deeply entrenched in the human psyche and heightened by the current economic context, is further stimulated by politicians and the media. The latter use hyperbolic accounts of foreigner 'invasions' and 'floods' to manipulate public consciousness and construe immigrants as enemies waiting to besiege their host countries. It is a fictional depiction that reinforces and feeds upon the original fear of alterity.

The details of this fictionalization process were exemplified by a case study: the alleged murder of Italian citizen Giovanna Reggiani by a Romanian immigrant of Roma origin in October 2007. At the time of the crime, the Italian public had already been exposed to statistics and news stories which associated Romanian immigrants with criminality. Through the extensive use of securitizing language and the adoption of emergency measures in response to the murder, Italian politicians encouraged the public's fear of immigrants in general and of Romanians in particular. Romanian workers (as well as Roma ethnics) were portrayed as dangerous intruders who posed a serious threat to Italian security. This skilful manipulation of public fears was also supported by media accounts, which assigned a symbolical dimension to the event by focusing on the nationalities of those involved. A similar tendency was at work in the Romanian press, which emphasized the Roma origin of the alleged criminal and brought into the foreground some of the pejorative connotations ascribed to this ethnic group in Romanian society.

The dimensions of the event were thus magnified to the point of spurring violent public reactions. At the same time, the supposed murderer, Romulus Mailat, was hastily sentenced to life in prison, despite a lack of solid evidence. The fairness of the trial was generally taken for granted: being both a Romanian and a Roma, Mailat was the perfect criminal. From an Italian perspective, he was a plausible perpetrator on account of his Romanian nationality, since in the mind of the Italian public there was a strong connection between Romanians and criminality. At the same time, he was an equally credible murderer from the vantage point of Romanians, who associated the Roma with criminality. It was a convincing fiction, created through generalization and hyperbole, one that satisfied the public need for a scapegoat and whose price was possibly an abusive conviction. Three years after his imprisonment, Mailat wrote: 'I'm like a needle in a haystack, you lose it but you are not interested in looking for it anymore'.[54] The haunting thought is that he might be right.

Notes

[1] Jean Delumeau, *Frica in Occident (secolele XIV-XVIII). O cetate asediata* [*Fear in the West (14th-18th Centuries). A City Surrounded*] (Bucuresti: Meridiane, 1986), 72-73.

[2] Ibid., 73-74.

[3] 'Far-Right Parties Sweep EU Polls', *Aljazeera Online*, 26 May 2014, viewed on 7 February 2015, http://www.aljazeera.com/news/europe/2014/05/far-right-parties-sweep-eu-polls-20145261436233584.html.

[4] Catherine E. Shoichet and Jim Boulden,'That "Earthquake" in Europe? It's Far-Right Gains in Parliament Elections', *CNN Online*, 26 May 2014, viewed on 7 February 2015, http://commonnewsupdate.com/?p=51962.

[5] Will Hutton, 'While the European Left Dithers, the Right Marches Menacingly On', *The Guardian Online*, 15 May 2014, viewed on 7 February 2015, http://www.theguardian.com/commentisfree/2011/may/15/will-hutton-populist-right-gaining-europe.

[6] Cas Mudde, 'The Far Right in the 2014 European Elections: Of Earthquakes, Cartels and Designer Fascists', *The Washington Post Online*, 30 May 2014, viewed on 7 February 2015, http://www.washingtonpost.com/blogs/monkey-cage/wp/2014/05/30/the-far-right-in-the-2014-european-elections-of-earthquakes-cartels-and-designer-fascists/.

[7] James Shields, *The Extreme Right in France: From Pétain to Le Pen* (New York: Routledge, 2007), 284.

[8] Jessica Elgot, 'European Elections: 9 Scariest Far-Right Parties Now in the European Parliament', *Huffington Post Online*, 28 May 2014, viewed on 7 February 2015, http://www.huffingtonpost.co.uk/2014/05/26/far-right-europe-election_n_5391873.html.

[9] Kashmira Gander and Oliver Wright, 'Ukip Election Posters: Nigel Farage Defends "Racist" Campaign Anti-Immigration Campaign ahead of Europe Elections', *The Independent Online*, 21 April 2014, viewed on 7 February 2015, http://www.independent.co.uk/news/uk/home-news/ukip-accused-of-scaremongering-in-antiimmigration-poster-campaign-ahead-of-european-elections-9273100.html.

[10] Elgot, 'European Elections'.

[11] Claude Lévi-Strauss, *Race and History* (Paris: Unesco, 1952), 11.

[12] Ulrich Beck, *Was ist Globalisierung. Irrtümer des Globalismus - Antworten auf Globalisierung* [*What is Globalization? Errors of Globalism - Answers to Globalization*] (Frankfurt am Main: Suhrkamp, 1997), 49.

[13] Ibid., 50.

[14] Ulrich Beck, 'Wie wird Demokratie im Zeitalter der Globalisierung möglich? Eine Einleitung'['How is Democracy Possible in the Age of Globalization? An Introduction'], *Politik der Globalisierung* [*The Politics of Globalization*], ed. Ulrich Beck (Suhrkamp: Frankfurt am Main, 1998), 7-66, 54.

[15] Régis Debray, *Éloge des frontières* [*Praise of Borders*] (Paris: Gallimard, 2010), 63.

[16] Chris Shore, 'European Union and the Politics of Culture,' *Brugesgroup.com*, 2001, viewed on 23 May 2014, http://www.brugesgroup.com/news.live?framed =1&article=13&keyword=0.

[17] Slawomir Sierakowski and Charles Taylor, 'The De-Politization of Politics', *Eurozine Online*, 10 November 2011, viewed on 10 February 2015, http://www.eurozine.com/articles/2011-11-10-sierakowski-en.html.

[18] Shore, 'European Union and the Politics of Culture'.

[19] Debray, *Éloge des frontières*, 18-19.

[20] Jeremy Harding, *Border Vigils: Keeping Migrants out of the Rich World* (London/New York: Verso, 2012), 75.

[21] Jef Huysmans, 'The European Union and the Securitization of Migration,' *Journal of Common Market Studies* 38, No. 5 (2000):, 751-777, 768-769.

[22] Ibid. 758.

[23] Vintila Mihailescu, 'Hannibal ante portas sau despre fictiunea migratiei' ['Hannibal ante portas or on the Fiction of Migration'], *Critic Atac Online*, 30 November 2011, viewed on 2 February 2015, http://www.criticatac.ro/11498/hannibal-ante-portas-sau-despre-fictiunea-migratiei/.

[24] Irina Angelescu, 'All New Migration Debates Commence in Rome: New Developments in the Securitization of Migration in the EU,' *Across Fading Borders: The Challenges of East-West Migration in the EU* (2008): 1-6, viewed on 23 May 2014, http://www.academia.edu/872035/All_New_Migration_Debates_Commence_in_R ome_New_Developments_in_the_Securitization_of_Migration_in_the_EU, 1.

[25] Huysmans, 'The European Union and the Securitization of Migration,' 759.

[26] Ibid., 760.

[27] Philippe Bourbeau, *The Securitization of Migration: A Study of Movement and Order* (London: Routledge, 2011), 102.

[28] Mihailescu, 'Hannibal ante portas sau despre fictiunea migratiei'.

[29] 'Romeni e violenza. 2007, un anno nero' ['Romanians and Violence: A Dark Year'], *La Repubblica Online*, 1 November 2007, viewed on 23 May 2014, http://www.repubblica.it/2007/10/sezioni/cronaca/tor-di-quinto/romeni-violenza/romeni-violenza.html.

[30] Antonieta M. Calabro, 'Omicidi, violenze, furti: il "caso romeno"' ['Homicides, Violence, Thefts: The "Romanian Case"'], *Corriere della Sera Online*, 23 February 2009, viewed on 23 May 2014, http://www.corriere.it/cronache/09_febbraio_23/calabro_d5e96f52-0189-11de-91dc-00144f02aabc.shtml.

[31] Bruno Persano, 'Roma, aggredita alla fermata del treno. E' in fin di vita, arrestano romeno' ['Rome, Attacked at the Train Station: As She Lies Dying, They Arrest Romanian Man'], *La Repubblica Online*, 31 October 2007, viewed on 23 May 2014, http://www.repubblica.it/2007/10/sezioni/cronaca/tor-di-quinto/tor-di-quinto/tor-di-quinto.html.

[32] Guglielmo Ragozzino, 'Supertestimoni incompatibili e inattendibili, Mailat o forse...' ['Incompatible, Implausible Main Witnesses: Mailat or Maybe...'], *Il Manifesto*, 5 July 2009, viewed on 23 May 2014, http://www.identitatearomaneasca.it/smf/index.php?topic=1168.0;wap2.

[33] Ibid.

[34] 'Avocatul lui Mailat: Daca a ucis-o, inseamna ca n-a atins-o' ['Mailat's Lawyer: If He Killed Her, It Means He Didn't Touch Her'], *EVZ Online*, 29 October 2008, viewed on 23 May 2014, http://www.evz.ro/avocatul-lui-mailat-daca-a-ucis-o-inseamna-ca-n-a-atins-o-826265.html.

[35] Angelescu, 'All New Migration Debates Commence in Rome,' 2.

[36] Ibid.

[37] Liana Milella and Giovanna Vitale, 'Romeni, scattano le espulsioni "Via i primi cinquemila"' ['Romanians, Expulsions Are Starting. "The First Five Thousand Sent Away"'], *La Repubblica Online*, 2 November 2007, viewed on 23 May 2014, http://www.repubblica.it/2007/10/sezioni/cronaca/tor-di-quinto/scattano-espulsioni/scattano-espulsioni.html.

[38] 'Via libera al decreto sulle espulsioni' ['Go-Ahead for Expulsion Decree'], *Corriere della Sera Online*, 31 October 2007, viewed on 23 May 2014, http://www.corriere.it/politica/07_ottobre_31/veltroni_sicurezza_pacchetto.shtml.

[39] John Hooper, 'Italian Woman's Murder Prompts Expulsion Threat to Romanians,' *The Guardian Online*, 2 November 2007, viewed on 23 May 2014, http://www.theguardian.com/world/2007/nov/02/italy.international.

[40] 'Berlusconi Calls for Ban on Romanian Workers,' *The New York Times Online*, November 4, 2007, viewed on 23 May 2014, http://www.nytimes.com/2007/11/04/world/europe/04ihtitaly.58184546.html?_r=0.

[41] Nando Sigona, 'Gypsies out of Italy!,' *Italy Today: The Sick Man of Europe*, eds. Andrea Mammone and Giuseppe A. Veltri (New York: Routledge, 2010), 143-157, 147.

[42] Tom Kington, 'Ex-Leader of Neo-Fascists Wins in Rome,' *The Guardian Online*, 29 April 2008, viewed on 23 May 2014, http://www.theguardian.com/world/2008/apr/29/italy.

[43] 'Disharmony and Tension,' *The Economist Online*, 8 November, 2007, viewed on 23 May 2014, http://www.economist.com/node/10105059.

[44] D. Mihai, 'Italienii isi fac singuri dreptate, Basescu sesizeaza Bruxelles-ul' ['Italians Take Justice into Their Own Hands, Basescu Notifies Brussels'], *Hotnews.ro*, viewed on 23 May 2014, http://www.hotnews.ro/stiri-arhiva-1006058-italienii-isi-fac-singuri-dreptate-basescu-sesizeaza-bruxelles.htm.

[45] 'Ministrul Adrian Cioroianu si-a pus in cap senatorii liberali' ['Minister Adrian Cioroianu Has Spurred the Criticism of Liberal Senators'], *EVZ Online*, 14 November 2007, viewed on 23 May 2014, http://www.evz.ro/ministrul-adrian-cioroianu-si-a-pus-in-cap-senatorii-liberali-468038.html.

[46] Lorenzo Guadagnucci, *Lavavetri* [*Window Cleaner*] (Milano: Terre di Mezzo, 2009), 86.

[47] Grazia Naletto, 'L'omicidio Reggiani' ['The Reggiani Homicide'], *Rapporto sul razzismo in Italia* [*A Report on Racism in Italy*], ed. Grazia Naletto (Roma: Manifestolibri, 2009), 64-68, 66.

[48] Ionut Codreanu and Nicoleta Fotiade, *Cazul Mailat in presa. Raport de analiza media (1-10 noiembrie 2007)* [*The Mailat Case in the Press. Media Analysis Report (1-10 November 2007)*] (Bucuresti: Agentia de Monitorizare a Presei, 2008), 41.

[49] Ibid., 39.
[50] Ibid., 41.
[51] 'Sotul femeii ucise, monument de durere' ['The Husband of the Murdered Woman, a Monument of Grief'], *EVZ Online*, 4 November 2007, viewed on 23 May 2014,
http://www.evz.ro/sotul-femeii-ucise-monument-de-durere-466814.html.
[52] Naletto, 'L'omicidio Reggiani' ['The Reggiani Homicide'], 68.
[53] Angelescu, 'All New Migration Debates Commence in Rome,' 2.
[54] '"Epopeea" lui Mailat: "Sunt ca un ac in carul cu fan"' ['Mailat's "Epic": "I'm like a Needle in a Haystack"'], *EVZ Online*, 18 June 2010, viewed on 23 May 2014,
http://www.evz.ro/epopeea-lui-mailat-sunt-ca-un-ac-in-carul-cu-fan-898515.html.

Bibliography

Angelescu, Irina. 'All New Migration Debates Commence in Rome: New Developments in the Securitization of Migration in the EU.' *Across Fading Borders: The Challenges of East-West Migration in the EU* (2008): 1-6. Viewed on 23 May 2014.
http://www.academia.edu/872035/All_New_Migration_Debates_Commence_in_R
ome_New_Developments_in_the_Securitization_of_Migration_in_the_EU.

Beck, Ulrich. *Was ist Globalisierung. Irrtümer des Globalismus: Antworten auf Globalisierung.* Frankfurt am Main: Suhrkamp, 1997.

Beck, Ulrich. 'Wie wird Demokratie im Zeitalter der Globalisierung möglich? Eine Einleitung.' *Politik der Globalisierung*, edited by Ulrich Beck, 7-66. Frankfurt am Main: Suhrkamp, 1998.

Bourbeau, Philippe. *The Securitization of Migration: A Study of Movement and Order.* London: Routledge, 2011.

Calabro, Antonieta M. 'Omicidi, violenze, furti: il "caso romeno".' *Corriere della Sera Online*, 23 February 2009. Viewed on 23 May 2014.
http://www.corriere.it/cronache/09_febbraio_23/calabro_d5e96f52-0189-11de
91dc-00144f02aabc.shtml.

Codreanu, Ionut and Nicoleta Fotiade. *Cazul Mailat in presa. Raport de analiza media (1-10 noiembrie 2007).* Bucuresti: Agentia de Monitorizare a Presei, 2008.

Debray, Régis, *Éloge des frontières*. Paris: Gallimard, 2010.

Delumeau, Jean. *Frica in Occident (secolele XIV-XVIII). O cetate asediata.* Bucuresti: Meridiane, 1986.

Elgot, Jessica. 'European Elections: 9 Scariest Far-Right Parties Now in the European Parliament.' *Huffington Post Online*, 28 May 2014. Viewed on 7 February 2015.
http://www.huffingtonpost.co.uk/2014/05/26/far-right-europe-election_n_5391873.html.

Gander, Kashmira and Oliver Wright. 'Ukip Election Posters: Nigel Farage Defends "Racist" Campaign Anti-Immigration Campaign ahead of Europe Elections.' *The Independent Online*, 21 April 2014. Viewed on 7 February 2015.
http://www.independent.co.uk/news/uk/home-news/ukip-accused-of-scaremongering-in-antiimmigration-poster-campaign-ahead-of-european-elections-9273100.html.

Guadagnucci, Lorenzo. *Lavavetri*. Milano: Terre di Mezzo, 2009.

Harding, Jeremy. *Border Vigils: Keeping Migrants out of the Rich World.* London/New York: Verso, 2012.

Hooper, John. 'Italian Woman's Murder Prompts Expulsion Threat to Romanians.' *The Guardian Online*, 2 November 2007. Viewed on May 23, 2014.
http://www.theguardian.com/world/2007/nov/02/italy.international.

Hutton, Will. 'While the European Left Dithers, the Right Marches Menacingly On.' *The Guardian Online*, 15 May 2014. Viewed on 7 February 2015.
http://www.theguardian.com/commentisfree/2011/may/15/will-hutton-populist-right-gaining-europe.

Huysmans, Jeff. 'The European Union and the Securitization of Migration.' *Journal of Common Market Studies*, Vol. 38, No. 5, December 2000: 751-777.

Kington, Tom. 'Ex-Leader of Neo-Fascists Wins in Rome.' *The Guardian Online*, 29 April 2008. Viewed on 23 May 2014.
http://www.theguardian.com/world/2008/apr/29/italy.

Lévi-Strauss, Claude. *Race and History*. Paris: Unesco, 1952.

Mihai, D. 'Italienii isi fac singuri dreptate, Basescu sesizeaza Bruxelles-ul.' *Hotnews.ro.* Viewed on 23 May 2014. http://www.hotnews.ro/stiri-arhiva-1006058-italienii-isi-fac-singuri-dreptate-basescu-sesizeaza-bruxelles.htm.

Mihailescu, Vintila. 'Hannibal ante portas sau despre fictiunea migratiei.' *Critic Atac Online,* 30 November 2011. Viewed on 2 February 2015. http://www.criticatac.ro/11498/hannibal-ante-portas-sau-despre-fictiunea-migratiei/.

Milella, Liana and Giovanna Vitale. 'Romeni, scattano le espulsioni "Via i primi cinquemila".' *La Repubblica Online,* 2 November 2007. Viewed on 23 May 2014. http://www.repubblica.it/2007/10/sezioni/cronaca/tor-di-quinto/scattano-espulsioni/scattano-espulsioni.html.

Mudde, Cas. 'The Far Right in the 2014 European Elections: Of Earthquakes, Cartels and Designer Fascists.' *The Washington Post Online,* 30 May 2014. Viewed on 7 February 2015. http://www.washingtonpost.com/blogs/monkey-cage/wp/2014/05/30/the-far-right-in-the-2014-european-elections-of-earthquakes-cartels-and-designer-fascists/.

Naletto, Grazia. 'L'omicidio Reggiani.' *Rapporto sul razzismo in Italia,* edited by Grazia Naletto, 64-68. Roma: Manifestolibri, 2009.

Persano, Bruno. 'Roma, aggredita alla fermata del treno. E' in fin di vita, arrestano romeno.' *La Repubblica Online,* 31 October 2007. Viewed on 23 May 2014. http://www.repubblica.it/2007/10/sezioni/cronaca/tor-di-quinto/tor-di-quinto/tor-di-quinto.html.

Ragozzino, Guglielmo. 'Supertestimoni incompatibili e inattendibili, Mailat o forse...' *Il Manifesto,* 5 July 2009. Viewed on 23 May 2014. http://www.identitatearomaneasca.it/smf/index.php?topic=1168.0;wap2.

Shields, James. *The Extreme Right in France: From Pétain to Le Pen.* New York: Routledge, 2007.

Shoichet, Catherine E. and Jim Boulden. 'That "Earthquake" in Europe? It's Far-Right Gains in Parliament Elections.' *CNN Online,* 26 May 2014. Viewed on 7 February 2015. http://commonnewsupdate.com/?p=51962.

Shore, Chris. 'European Union and the Politics of Culture.' *Brugesgroup.com*, 2001. Viewed on 23 May 2014. http://www.brugesgroup.com/news.live?framed.

Sierakowski, Slawomir and Charles Taylor. 'The De-Politization of Politics.' *Eurozine Online*, 10 November 2011. Viewed on 10 February 2015. http://www.eurozine.com/articles/2011-11-10-sierakowski-en.html.

Sigona, Nando. 'Gypsies out of Italy!' *Italy Today: The Sick Man of Europe*, edited by Andrea Mammone and Giuseppe A. Veltri, 143-157. New York: Routledge, 2010.

Travis, Alan. 'Number of Romanian and Bulgarian Workers in UK Falls.' *The Guardian Online*, 14 May 2014. Viewed on 23 May 2014. http://www.theguardian.com/uk-news/2014/may/14/number-romanian-bulgarian-workers-falls-border-controls.

———. 'Avocatul lui Mailat: Daca a ucis-o, inseamna ca n-a atins-o.' *EVZ Online*, 29 October 2008. Viewed on 23 May 2014. http://www.evz.ro/avocatul-lui-mailat-daca-a-ucis-o-inseamna-ca-n-a-atins-o- 826265.html.

———. 'Berlusconi Calls for Ban on Romanian Workers.' *The New York Times Online*, November 4, 2007. Viewed on 23 May 2014. http://www.nytimes.com/2007/11/04/world/europe/04ihtitaly.58184546.html?_r=0.

———. 'Disharmony and Tension.' *The Economist Online*, 8 November 2007. Viewed on 23 May 2014. http://www.economist.com/node/10105059.

———. '"Epopeea" lui Mailat: "Sunt ca un ac in carul cu fan".' *EVZ Online*, 18 June 2010. Viewed on 23 May 2014. http://www.evz.ro/epopeea-lui-mailat-sunt-ca-un-ac-in-carul-cu-fan-898515.html.

———. 'Far-Right Parties Sweep EU Polls.' *Aljazeera Online*, 26 May 2014. Viewed on 7 February 2015. http://www.aljazeera.com/news/europe/2014/05/far-right-parties-sweep-eu-polls-20145261436233584.html.

———. 'Ministrul Adrian Cioroianu si-a pus in cap senatorii liberali.' *EVZ Online*, 14 November 2007. Viewed on 23 May 2014. http://www.evz.ro/ministrul-adrian-cioroianu-si-a-pus-in-cap-senatorii-liberali-468038.html.

————. 'Romeni e violenza. 2007, un anno nero.' *La Repubblica Online*, 1 November 2007. Viewed on 23 May 2014. http://www.repubblica.it/2007/10/sezioni/cronaca/tor-di-quinto/romeni-violenza/romeni-violenza.html.

————. 'Sotul femeii ucise, monument de durere.' *EVZ Online*, 4 November 2007. Viewed on 23 May 2014. http://www.evz.ro/sotul-femeii-ucise-monument-de-durere-466814.html.

————. 'Via libera al decreto sulle espulsioni.' *Corriere della Sera Online*, 31 October 2007. Viewed on 23 May 2014. http://www.corriere.it/politica/07_ottobre_31/veltroni_sicurezza_pacchetto.shtml.

Stefania Alina Cherata is a PhD student at the University of Jena, Germany. Her main research focus is on the study of metaphor, but she also takes great interest in interdisciplinary approaches to language and culture.

The Case of Transnistria in the Context of the Russian Eurasian Union Project

Agnieszka Konopelko

Abstract
Following the Crimean case authorities of the Pridnestrovian Moldavian Republic (Transnistria, Transdniestria), unrecognized by the UN declared autonymity as a territorial unit, and appealed to the Russian parliament for integration with the Russian Federation territory. This ultimately would mean secession from the Republic of Moldova. The request aptly fits in with Putin's new doctrine of a foreign and security policies which seek to reintegrate the post-Soviet area and restore the unity of the 'Russian-speaking community.' Under this specific rhetoric (protection of the Russians' rights, political stabilization), aimed at the strengthening of federalism and incorporation to Custom Union, Russia uses its instruments of pressure such as: a blockade of goods imported from Moldova, repression of Moldavian migrant labour, or a propaganda war bent on fomenting separatism. Moldova, like the Ukraine and the South Caucasus countries is a landlocked country geopolitically and geostrategically situated between the European Union and Russia. Thus, Transnistria is an object of many fears and uncertainties both within Moldavian territory and outside the region. The author examines and analyses the current situation of the conflicted region not only in the context of Moldova anxieties about the further integration with the EU but also from the point of view of the Gagauzia (autonomous region of Moldova) will for separatism, the Ukrainian fears of the eastern regions' separatism, Romanian anxieties about Romanian-speaking minority in Moldova and finally the EU concerns about instability in the post-Soviet area and the eastern border of Europe. The author attempts to answer the questions of the future scenario of the Transnistrian conflict taking into account Putin's new strategy and internal conflicts especially in the light of multi-vector integration aspirations and the Russian pressure.

Key Words: Transnistria, Moldova, Eurasia, Putin's doctrine, 'hybrid war,' frozen conflicts.

*****

1. Introduction

The former Soviet Union area is contrastive and unpredictable. It has experienced various ethnic, language, religion and territorial conflicts. Many of them resolved by military means. Thus, many fears and anxieties result from a lack of a sense of stability both in political and security dimensions as well as economic and social aspects. The Ukrainian crisis showed that these fears were not causeless.

The liminal moments between peace and war described by Ismee Tames[1] have evolved dynamically towards the outright war conflict in the Eastern Ukraine and forced many civilians to leave the country. Thus, it is hard to disagree with professor Zbigniew Brzezinski that the regional Eurasian strategy of the Russian elites should not be ignored:

> Regrettably, the imperial impulse remains strong and even appears to be strengthening. This is not only a matter of political rhetoric. Particularly troubling is the growing assertiveness of the Russian military in the effort to retain or regain control over the old Soviet empire. Initially, these efforts may have been the spontaneous acts of rogue military commanders in the field. However, military self-assertion in such places as Moldova, Crimea, Ossetia, Georgia ..., perpetuates imperial enclaves on the outer edges of the former empire.[2]

The conflict in Transnistria concerns multiple facets rooted in a complicated, embroiled history and geopolitical situation. According to Ministry of Foreign Affairs of Pridnestrovian Moldavian Republic (PMR) in 2009 the total population of Transnistria equalled 555.000, with three major ethnic groups: Moldovans (31.9%), Russians (30.3%) and Ukrainians (28.8%).[3]

In 1990 by the Declaration of Sovereignty the Transnistrian Soviet Socialist Republic proclaimed its secession from the Moldavian Soviet Socialist Republic. As the Soviet Union began to collapse in 1991 and Moldova declared its independence, pro-Russian separatists in Transnistria, fearing that Moldova could unite with neighbouring Romania, declared independence from Moldova and established the Pridnestrovian Moldavian Republic under an authoritarian presidential system. With weapons and other assistance from the Russian army, it was involved in a military conflict with Moldova. In June 1992 with Russian support, PMR maintained its independence and Moldova had to put up with ceasefire and creation of a demilitarized security zone. A new Moldavian constitution in 1994 gave the territory substantial autonomy, but the conflict remains unresolved.[4]

Declaration of independence of Pridnestrovian Moldavian Republic was not recognized by the United Nations and international community. According to international law it breaks a principle of territorial integrity of Moldova and the inviolability of its borders.

Some politicians and researchers point at the declaration of independence of Kosovo as a direct determinant, or even the formal legal rationale of the Transnistrian authorities request to the United Nations for the recognition of the self-proclaimed republic.

Vladimir Putin described this in his address to the State Duma on 18 March 2014, as:

> A precedent our western colleagues created with their own hands
> ... when they agreed that the unilateral separation of Kosovo
> from Serbia, exactly what Crimea is doing now, was legitimate
> and did not require any permission from the country's central
> authorities.[5]

Despite the fact that the International Court of Justice in its judgement recognised the unilateral declaration of Kosovo's independence from Serbia legal, it simultaneously stated that this decision was exceptional, refers exclusively to Kosovo and should not make a precedence for other entities in the world. Although the international law does not introduce a ban on independence declarations (self-determination principle), it leaves the recognition of new entities a subject of sovereign decisions of particular states.[6]

The Deputy Prime Minister of Moldova, Victor Osipov in 2010 stressed that 'the UN does not recognize the independence, it includes in its list only the states whose independence is already recognized.'[7]

2. Roots of the Moldova's Fears

So far, the leaders of Transnistrian political elites have not declared an integration with the Russian Federation but 'only' an independence. Recently we can observe a change in their rhetoric, especially of main parliamentary party *The Renewal* [*Obnovleniye*], conflicted with Yevgeny Shevchuk – President of Transnistria) and closer integration with *New Russia*.

New Russia [*Novorossiya*], historical part of Imperial Russia, refers to some regions of southern and eastern Ukraine (Kharkov, Lugansk, Donetsk, Kherson, Nikolayev and Odessa). In the tsarist days Novorossiysk was the centre of this territory. On 1 April 2014 Vladimir Putin stated that the aforementioned region was not included by the Soviet authorities as part of the Ukraine, while in the current situation the Russian minority needs help to protect its rights.[8]

It is worth noting that according to 2014 polls, conducted by the Russian research organization Levada Center and Kiev International Institute of Sociology, the majority of respondents (in the Ukraine – 68%, in Russia – 59%) voted for independence of the Ukraine and the Russian Federation but with open borders without visas and customs. Integration with Russia into a single state was supported by 12% of respondents in the Ukraine. Most of the supporters voted in the eastern (26%) and the southern (19%) regions.[9]

To enhance a symbolic and institutional Russian presence in the region, in November 2012 the leader of Transnistria Yevgeny Shevchuk signed a new measure of a foreign policy with the main priorities being full economic, cultural and political integration with the Custom Union of Russia, Belarus and Kazakhstan and ultimately the Eurasian Union.[10]

Upon the Transnistrian policy of Eurasian integration the *Eurasian Pridnestrovie* project set a goal to take part in creation of the new Eurasian supranational union. The project was designed to create the Internet information-analytical media portal. Such information resource on the processes of the Eurasian integration focuses on a close cooperation with the countries of the Common Economic Space and the Customs Union in the field of economy and trade, education and culture, environment and tourism. The project also involves conducting research, media monitoring, expert interviews, creation of an Internet and television Eurasian space and supplying information for regional and central Russian mass media.[11]

Recently, President Yevgeny Shevchuk clearly opts for integration of Transnistria with Russia. On 9 May 2014 he underlined that 'Transnistrian land became a part of the Russian Empire more than two hundred years ago'[12] and the majority of inhabitants show support for unification with Russia. During a recent interviews Shevchuk stated that 'it is necessary for Transnistria to be recognized as independent state and then integrate with Russia.'[13]

Last 'independence' referendum in Transnistria was held in 2006. More than 97% of voters supported the independence of Transnistria and the subsequent free association with the Russian Federation. Simultaneously, 94.9% of the voters were against becoming a part of Moldova.[14]

In fact, we can call it rather a popularity poll than a real democratic referendum. According to Oazu Nantoi, Program Director of the Institute for Public Policy in Chisinau:

> It was not a referendum, but a spectacle organized by security services, where people were driven like so much sheep to the polls, while the government invented figures that would please the Kremlin. In a democratic country, a referendum may only be held by free citizens, but not in an occupied territory. Everything that happens in an occupied territory is illegitimate.[15]

Many various opinion polls show that most Moldovans are indifferent towards the Transnistria region. For the vast majority, the issue ranks as the ninth or tenth most important priority for the population of Moldova proper. Besides, many of new generation of Moldovans and Transnistrians have not experienced living in a united society within Moldova territory.

In 2009-2010 professors Gerard Toal and John O'Loughlin conducted survey in Abkhazia, South Ossetia and Transnistria on how citizens in these regions felt about Russia. In Transnistria only 40% of Moldovans and 50% of Ukrainians and

Russians minorities preferred integration with Russia. In turn, more than 30% people showed support for independence.[16]

In June 2014, research company IRI Baltic Surveys/The Gallup Organization conducted a survey interviewing residents of Moldova (excluding Transnistria). One of the questions was 'What do you think the future of Transnistria should be?' The substantial majority supported for full unification of Transnistria with Moldova (67%) or autonomy within Moldova (16%) and only 7% integration with Russia and 6% being independent.[17]

Transnistrian steps towards full independence are strengthened by the Gagauzian will for separatism. Gagauzia consists of four regions of southern Moldova and covers 5% of Moldavian territory. In 1990 in response to Moldova's Declaration of Sovereignty, congress of representatives of the Gagauz minority announced the formation of a 'Republic of Gagauzia.' In 1994 an Autonomous Territorial Unit of Gagauzia in Moldova was established as a special administrative area of southern Moldova.[18]

Upon the 2003 amendment, the Constitution of the Republic of Moldova acknowledged the autonomous status of a territorial unit of Gagauzia. With respect of the territorial integrity of Moldova it recognized its autonomous representative and executive bodies and right to legislative initiative. In turn, a status of the Transnistria territory (left bank of the Dniester River) has not been defined by the constitution. Due to complicated situation of the territory the constitution introduced a general regulation for the future assignment of the possible special form and conditions of its autonomy.[19]

On 2 February 2014, the Autonomous Territorial Unit of Gagauzia held two referendums on a future scenario. In the first, 98.5% of voters supported joining the Custom Union of Belarus, Kazakhstan and the Russian Federation. In the second, 98% opposed the further integration with the EU.[20]

It seems that the success in the polls was determined by the Russian propaganda and the anxieties of a possible union of Moldova and Romania. Moscow increased its activities on strengthening of Transnitrian and Gagauzian separatism. Moreover, in the context of the Ukrainian crisis described by the politicians, media and the observers as a 'hybrid war' some of the officials began to compare the Ukrainian scenario to the case of Moldova and Transnistria.

In theory, a term 'hybrid war' or 'hybrid warfare' is defined as 'a fused mix of conventional weapons, irregular tactics, terrorism and criminal behaviour in the battle space to obtain their political objectives'[21] or a combination of the 'political, military, economic, social and information means.'[22]

A new concept of the 'hybrid war' appeared in the Russian approach towards the Crimea and the Eastern Ukraine. The strategy developed the blended conventional hostile actions (hard power) and non-military means (soft power) with a great support of the Russian media (propaganda).

Andriy Parubiy, the former Secretary of Ukraine's Council for Security and Defense, concluded that:

> this is a so-called new type of war, a hybrid war, where armies do not always take on the role of direct aggressor. Instead, they serve to intimidate, while imported sabotage groups do the fighting together with local extremists and criminal gangs fight on the ground.[23]

In September 2014 during the meeting of the Atlantic Council, Philip Breedlove, U.S. Air Force General and the head of the NATO forces in Europe stated that Russia began to use the scenario of the 'hybrid war' against Moldova. The Russian troops or 'little green men' started military exercises and recruitment of the local youth in Transnistria region. Breedlove noted:

> To the little green men thing, we've clearly now seen the script play out in Crimea, we've seen the script play out in eastern Ukraine. We're beginning to see some of the script in Moldova and Transnistria.[24]

Recently, the Transnistria region irrespective of Moldavian-Russian relations has obtained economic privileges including exclusion of Gagauzian wines from the Russian embargo on Moldova and the announcement of receiving preferential prices for Russian gas. Moscow goal is to impose a model of federalization in Moldova and Transnistria.[25]

Russia's steps regarding Transnistria should also be perceived in the context by which Moscow attempts to weaken Moldova and EU rapprochement thanks to a free trade agreement and pressure from Moscow on Moldova accession to the Custom Union.

On 27 June 2014, during the EU Summit, Moldova and Georgia ceased the association agreements with the EU. According to the 'Association Agreement between the European Union and the European Atomic Energy Community and their Member States, of the one part, and the Republic of Moldova, of the other part,' one of the main political goals is:

> a sustainable solution of the Transnistrian issue, in full respect of the sovereignty and territorial integrity of the Republic of Moldova ... inviolability of borders and independence .... The Parties shall enhance practical cooperation in conflict prevention and crisis management, in particular with a view to the possible participation of the Republic of Moldova in EU-led civilian and military crisis management operations as well as relevant

exercises and training, on a case-by-case basis and following possible invitation by the EU.[26]

We can expect that the worsening economic-social situation in Transnistria can be used by Russian propaganda to prove that the agreements signed by Chisinau will lead to a full economic blockade of the region which ultimately may cause an economic collapse of Transnistria.

Due to EU and NATO concerns about instability in this post-Soviet area and the eastern border of Europe, the European Union established on 30 November 2005 the EU Border Assistance Mission (EUBAM) on the Ukrainian-Moldavian border. The border management programme aims to combat illegal trade flows, drug, arms trafficking, the smuggling of humans and uranium, as well as organized crime.[27]

At the same time, the EUBAM programme managed to improve the procedures of crossing the border in the area of Euroregion Dniester through the visa liberalization, updating technological schemes of border crossing points and the development of the techniques for systematic risk identification.[28]

An additional problem has arisen between Romanian-language schools in Transnistria and Russian-language schools in the rest of Moldova. On both sides of Dniester each language group fears discrimination by authorities in Chisinau and Tiraspol. Some fears have been justified by occasional and provocative school closures and curriculum changes.[29]

The anxieties held by the Romanian-speaking minority in Moldova appear in the context of Moldavian national identity and reunification of Moldova and Romania. The prospect of unification was totally unthinkable for Moldova's minorities and became one of the driving motivations for the Transnistrian and Gagauz secession.

According to the Gallup Institute survey from 2011, nearly 60% of voters were against becoming a part of Romania. Simultaneously, more than 30% of the voters supported the reunification of the Republic of Moldova with Romania. In turn, the 2014 survey of the Romanian Centre of Strategic Studies showed that 52% of voters supported joining Romania and 32% opposed the reunification of Moldova and Romania (Table 1).

Moldavian Constitutional Court accepted Romanian language as an official state language in Moldova, next to the Moldavian language. However, Moldavian language is regarded by linguists as identical with Romanian, or as a Romanian dialect but not a separate language. In the context of identity conflict in Moldova that divides a political stage into supporters of 'Moldovianism' ('Moldovans' refer to the separate nation) and 'unionists' ('Moldovans' are the part of the Romanian nation), and this reflects the third ideological stream. It recognizes a historical, cultural and linguistic community of Moldovans and Romanians but unlike the 'unionists' it does not postulate an integration but a further existence of the Moldavian state.[30]

Table 1: Results of the Gallup Institute and the Romanian Centre of Strategic Studies surveys on the reunification of Moldova and Romania.[31]

	Do you support or oppose the reunification of the Republic of Moldova with Romania? 2011 (Gallup Institute survey)	Do you support or oppose the reunification of the Republic of Moldova with Romania? 2014 (Romanian Centre of Strategic Studies survey)
Fully support	11%	27%
Somewhat support	20%	25%
Fully oppose	43%	12%
Somewhat oppose	16%	20%
No answer	10%	16%

Source: 'Moldova National Voter Study', 20 August – 2 September 2011, IRI Baltic Surveys/The Gallup Organization, 2011. MEDIAFAX.ro, http://www.mediafax.ro.

3. Putin's Vison of a New *Eurasia*

So far, in Putin's rhetoric we have been introduced to the term *Rossijskij narod* [Russian people] during the process of a nation-building state. It refers to all citizens of Russia in the scope of its territory irrespective of their ethnic origin (political nation). A social, linguistic and cultural basis of the Russian citizens nation is *Russkij narod* [Russian nation].[32]

Aleksander Dugin and Igor Panarin, the well-known geopolitical advisors in Russia, proposed a new concept of the term *Eurasia*. The Eurasianism as a global trend, a global-scale strategy or a global idea of the 'nation-states' rejects the centralized model of the world (Atlantism, Americanism) and determines multipolar areas including ethnic, cultural, religious and administrative factors. Dugin and Panarin see the Eurasianism as the philosophy of the post-Soviet territory integration on a democratic, non-violent, and voluntary basis without domination of any religious or ethnic group.[33]

In the context of the *Russkij Mir* (the territory of the former Soviet Union) Igor Panarin opts for the creation of the *Eurasian Russia* based on free integration, the common values, strong states, social partnership and the national tradition.[34]

A new Putin's doctrine of a foreign and security policy emphasizes not only reintegration of the post-Soviet area but also restoration of the unity of the 'Russian-speaking community.' The aforementioned community (*Russkij Mir*) identifies itself with the Russian language, Orthodox religion, culture and common values irrespective of citizenship and ethnic origin.[35]

As we can notice such concept moves beyond the territorial boundaries and bases on the cultural and ethnic values. A new approach and the new mechanisms in the context of the European integration are presented by Alina Cherata in her contribution to discussion on the European fears and anxieties.[36]

In Russian media there are often visible arguments for the necessity of protection of the Russians' rights, political stabilization, and good-neighbourliness and national interest. On 18 March 2014, Vladimir Putin stated:

> Russians are one of the largest "divided nations" in the world. I expect that the citizens of Germany will also support the aspiration of the Russians, of historical Russia, to restore unity. Millions of Russians and Russian-speaking people live in Ukraine and will continue to do so. Russia will always defend their interests using political, diplomatic and legal means.[37]

Besides, recently we can observe in Putin's speeches some references to the new arguments, such as: justice, truth and national will.[38]

> Crimea has always been an inseparable part of Russia. This firm conviction is based on truth and justice and was passed from generation to generation ... Russia is an independent, active participant in international affairs; like other countries, it has its own national interests...Russia's foreign policy position on this matter drew its firmness from the will of millions of our people, our national unity ... and any decision here can be based only on the people's will.[39]

Under this specific rhetoric the Kremlin uses many pressure instruments to influence the post-Soviet region including Moldova.

One of the main security goals of the Russian leaders is maintenance of military presence in the Transnistrian region and leaving of Moldova excluded from NATO. According to many analysts, Transnistria exists thanks to economic, financial, military and political support of the Russian Federation. Almost 1,200 Russian troops remain in Transnistria as part of a trilateral Russian -Moldovan-Transnistrian peace-keeping operation under the terms of the 21 July 1992 Moscow Agreement.[40] This so-called Operational Group of Russian Troops is a successor to the Soviet 14th Army.

> However, the joint peacekeeping force was established and has been operated in a way that violates internationally accepted

norms and principles of peacekeeping by using military forces of
direct participants in the conflict, and therefore cannot be seen as
neutral and impartial.[41]

The so-called 'Kozak Memorandum' in 2003 was the Russian plan for the
settlement of the Dniester conflict by means of federalization of Moldova
including a long-term Russian military presence. The plan set up an 'asymmetric
federalization' which meant maximization of the Transnistria influence on federal
authorities and minimization of the federal influence on Transnistria. Due to its
contradiction with the Moldavian constitution President Voronin declined to sign
the memorandum.[42] By an institutional approach of regional integration one of
Moscow's objectives was to engage Moldova, the Ukraine and the other post-
Soviet countries into the Eurasian Union project.

In 2011, the presidents of Russia, Belarus and Kazakhstan signed an agreement
on the Eurasian Economic Union (EEU) for its creation in 2015. The official
agreement was signed on 29 May 2014. According to Moscow the EEU plans to
enlarge almost all CIS (Commonwealth of Independent States) countries. It could
be a counterweight to the European Union and would be based on the Custom
Union.[43]

There is no doubt that the main beneficiary of the union will be Russia. Critics
of the Eurasian integration model notice that it will deepen political and economic
dependence by member states on Russia and limit their real sovereignty. Moreover,
such a union does not ensure regional stabilization due to Russia's involvement in
conflicts between the former Soviet republics.

Community for Democracy and Rights of Nations created in 2006 on the basis
of the declaration of three quasi states: Transnistria, Abkhazia and South Ossetia is
supported by the Russian Federation, as well. The organization concentrates not
only on international economic and political cooperation but also on closer
integration and recognition by international community of its members' sovereign
statehood.[44] Some experts maintain that the aforementioned initiative is determined
by development of the GUAM association and its transformation into more
integrated Organization for Democracy and Economic Development-GUAM.
GUAM is negatively perceived by Russia as the US instrument of the aggressive
policy on the Commonwealth of Independent States territory. Moreover, one of the
GUAM objectives is the solution of the territorial conflicts taking into account
territorial integrity.[45]

It is hard to disagree with Katarzyna Czerewacz-Filipowicz's opinion that the
Russian Federation enhances its influence and dominance in the region in the name
of integration policy with a support of many different instruments.[46] Russia became
the main trading partner of the Pridnestrovian Moldavian Republic. A large
dependence of the Transnistrian trade on the import of the Russian commodities
may be particularly evident (Table 2).[47]

Table 2: Major trading partners of the Pridnestrovian Moldavian Republic
in 2009-2013 (in US dol.)

Export partners					
	2009	2010	2011	2012	2013
Moldova	192.3	202.9	214.3	248.8	234.5
Russia	116.4	104.3	162.8	154.7	103.1
Italy	50.8	58.4	59.3	46.8	49.7
Ukraine	17.9	31.2	70.6	59.6	46.1
Romania	42.4	41.0	74.3	103.1	45.2
Germany	26.6	38.2	33.2	27.4	29.8
Import partners					
	2009	2010	2011	2012	2013
Russia	520.0	566.6	784.1	911.9	707.3
Ukraine	211.1	192.5	277.7	222.7	288.9
Belarus	53.9	60.7	99.4	108.4	107.3
Germany	48.1	61.8	93.6	89.0	95.1
Moldova	24.9	44.0	85.9	124.9	83.1
Italy	26.6	23.0	31.5	35.6	45.8

Source: Статистический Ежегодник 2014, Государственная Служба Статистики Приднестровской
Молдавской Республики, Тирасполь 2014.
Statistical Yearbook 2014, The National Statistical Service of the Pridnestrovian Moldavian Republic,
Tiraspol 2014.

It should be noted that due to the nature of the trade, differences in economic potential and a central strategic location of Russia the aforementioned integration strengthens rather bilateral economic relations of the post-Soviet countries with the Russian Federation than a multilateral cooperation within regional agreements.[48]

The Russian Federation became the greatest foreign investor in Moldova. At the end of 2012 the Russian investments noted nearly 23% of the total foreign direct investments. Similarly, in 2014 most of the Moldovan bank sector (70%) remained under control of the Russian capital.[49]

Moldova has no access to its own gas sources. Gazprom is the sole supplier of gas to Transnistria. The Moldovagaz company responsible for gas purchase and gas main management in Moldova belongs to Russia's Gazprom. Chisinau has only 35% of shares. Transnistria consumes more than 2/3 of gas delivered by Gazprom to Moldova. As of mid-2012, Transnistria's debt to Gazprom, the Russian natural gas supplier, stood at 3.8 billion dollars. This is almost double the 2 billion dollars gas debt owed by Ukraine to Russia.[50]

In September 2012 the Russian Deputy Prime Minister and a special representative 'on Transnistria,' Dmitrij Rogozin during his visit in Chisinau warned Moldova that further rapprochement with the EU will have a negative influence on the Russian-Moldavian trade and would force Russia to revise agreements and contribute to a reduction of labour possibilities for Moldovans in Russia. He stated that 'if Moldova will not recognize Transnistria, then it means that the gas consumed by Transnistria belongs – is Moldova's debt, and Moldova should pay for it.'[51]

The income from labour migrants have a significant importance for Moldavian economy. Almost half of 700-800 thousands Moldavian citizens (legally or illegally) working abroad is employed in Russia. More than 200,000 residents of Transnistria hold Russian passports and a vast majority receive their pensions from Russia. Between 66 and 86% of a total amount of migrant remittances, 184 mln dollars, comes from Transnistrian labourers in Russia.[52]

According to official data of the National Bureau of Statistics of the Republic of Moldova in 2013 more than 332,500 of Moldovans emigrated abroad to work or look for work abroad. Most of Moldavian labour force (223,600) immigrated to the Russian Federation (Table 3).[53]

Table 3: Moldavian labour force migration by country of destination in 2009-2013 (in thousands)

	2009	2010	2011	2012	2013
Total	294.9	311.0	316.9	328.3	332.5
Russia	177.2	191.9	204.8	223.4	223.6
Italy	54.8	58.6	58.4	54.9	50.7
Turkey	8.4	9.0	7.4	5.8	7.5
Israel	8.4	8.2	6.4	7.9	7.1
Ukraine	8.6	6.5	5.1	3.9	5.4
Portugal	6.4	5.1	4.4	3.2	4.1
Other countries	25.6	26.9	25.6	24.1	28.9

Source: National Bureau of Statistics of the Republic of Moldova.

In contrast to Russia's extension of citizenship to Russian-speaking residents of Transnistria, in 2013 6,900 Moldavian citizens were denied access for entry into Russia. Additionally, in 2014 Russia did not renew work permits for Moldavian workers. In response to Moldova ratification of the association agreement in June 2014, Russia prohibited importation of any Moldavian fruits or vegetables (according to Moldavian Ministry of Agriculture it will bring 80 million euros of loss). Previously, it imposed a blockade on goods imported from Moldova (mainly Moldavian wine). It was especially acute in terms of the sale of Moldavian alcohol products to Russia that reached 60 million dollars (3% of Moldavian export and 30% of wine export).[54]

According to Vitaly Ignatiev, Deputy Minister of Foreign Affairs of Pridnestrovian Moldavian Republic the population of Moldova and Transnistria became the main hostage of the policies within the negotiation process. Such opinion results from:

> the introduction of the Moldovan side of discriminatory import excise taxes, refusal to issue phytosanitary certificates of the Moldovan standard required for the transit of Pridnestrovian goods through Ukraine, intensification of repressive mechanism of initiation of criminal cases against officials of Pridnestrovie, illegal detentions and arrests of our citizens.[55]

4. Conclusions

It should be noted that Moldova is not a priority partner for Moscow. The country is poor, landlocked, and Romanian-speaking, with few natural resources and very little geostrategic value. Thus, Transnistria is not a strategic land for Russia. Crimea and Ukraine are treated by Russia as a natural influence zone. Moldova is rather perceived as a historical part of Romania. However, in 2012 Russian President Dmitry Medvedev appointed Deputy Prime Minister Dmitry Rogozin as special representative on Moldova's breakaway republic of Transnistria. This step was negatively perceived in Moldova and the West. In Chisinau some people emphasize that the appointment of a special representative on Transnistria is nothing else but an establishment of foreign control over the part of sovereign territory of the Republic of Moldova, and a direct threat towards its statehood.

In fact, the territory of Transnistria remains under the effective control of the Pridnestrovian Moldavian Republic authorities that are not legitimized by any state but consequently aim at closer integration with Russia or *Novorossiya*.

Since 2005, the Transnistrian settlement talks have been held in the 5+2 format that includes the conflicted sides (Transnistria and Moldova), mediators (the OSCE, Russia, and Ukraine) and observers (the European Union and the United States). The goal of the talks is a final and comprehensive settlement of the Transnistrian conflict, finding a special status for Transnistria and respecting the territorial integrity and sovereignty of Moldova.[56]

For Transnistria the main goals of the talks under negotiations 5+2 concern the recognition of its sovereign statehood on an international stage and possibility of its accession to the Russian integration project of *Eurasian Union*.

Although, ten official meetings were held between 2012 and 2013, and two so far in 2014, no progress has been made. The latter talks focused on restoring commercial, banking, and telecommunications links between Transnistria and the rest of Moldova, and the reopening of freight rail routes across the Dniester.

However, while dialogue was maintained, no negotiations have taken place on the political status of Transnistria.[57]

In 2010 German Chancellor Angela Merkel and the Russian President Dmitry Medvedev signed the 'Meseberg Memorandum' and established the EU-Russia Political and Security Committee on ministerial level. This diplomatic initiative aimed to bring the EU and Russia to closer cooperation towards a resolution of the Transnistria conflict with a view to achieve progress within the established 5+2 format.[58]

The so-called 'Meseberg Process' failed to change Russia's approach to the conflict.[59] Moreover it should be emphasized that the German negotiations were not coordinated with the other European partners. However, the German initiative accelerated a positive dynamic in 5+2 negotiations on Transnistria conflict resolution.

It is obvious that in a long term perspective a *status quo* of Transnistria will not be a desirable solution, especially in terms of a 'new' Kremlin's doctrine of reintegration of the Soviet empire and the integration of Russian-speaking community. The Ukrainian case proves a consequent strategy of the Russian influence zone restoration and insufficiency of Western soft-power diplomacy. Chisinau is interested to maintain the dialogue with Tiraspol. Of course, the European Union should not push for a quick solution to the conflict. Wise conflict resolution will require a mutual political will, clear vison, and transparent information. Further, deeper integration of Moldova (including Transnistria) with the EU and NATO and democratization of its institutions and society would be a real alternative for the common future. Ambassador Jennifer Brush, former Head of the Organization for Security and Co-operation in Europe Mission to Moldova underlines that:

> We are going through tumultuous and difficult times in the region. There is change in the air, along with the fear and uncertainty which sometimes accompanies change in the absence of a convincingly articulated vision of the future. The first step towards building trust and confidence is overcoming fear. In a region where conflict has been woven into the fabric of history over the course of centuries, building trust is especially challenging.[60]

Acknowledgment:
The project has been financed from the National Science Centre funds awarded on the basis of Decision DEC-2011/03/B/HS4/05/930.

Notes

[1] Ismee Tames, 'Expecting War in Europe: Fears and Anxieties about War,' in *Fears and Anxieties in the 21st Century: The European Context and Beyond*, ed. Catalin Ghita and Robert Beshara (*Oxford: Inter-Disciplinary Press, 2015*).

[2] Zbigniew Brzeziński, 'The Premature Partnership,' *Foreign Affairs* 73/2 (1994): 72.

[3] Ministry of Foreign Affairs of Pridnestrovian Moldavian Republic, viewed on 2 February 2015, http://mfa-pmr.org/en.

[4] Freedom House, 'Freedom in the World 2013. Transnistria,' viewed on 15 August 2014, http://www.freedomhouse.org/report/freedomworld/2013/transnistria#.U85SoLF9b KE.

[5] 'Address by President of the Russian Federation,' *The Kremlin* website, 18 March 2014, viewed on 26 June 2014, http://eng.kremlin.ru/transcripts/6889.

[6] International Court of Justice, 'Accordance with International Law of the Unilateral Declaration of Independence in Respect of Kosovo (Request for Advisory Opinion),' viewed on 19 June 2014, http://www.icj-cij.org/docket/index.php?p1=3&p2=4&k=21&case=141& code=kos&p3=4.

[7] Anonymous, 'Transnistria's Appeal for Recognition to United Nations is Illogical,' *Moldova.org* website, viewed on 2 September 2014, http://www.moldova.org/transnistrias-appeal-for-recognition-to-united-nations-is-illogical-211282-eng.

[8] Paul Sonne, 'With *Novorossiya* Putin Plays the Name Game with Ukraine,' *The Wall Street Journal*, viewed on 17 January 2015, http://www.wsj.com/articles/with-novorossiya-putin-plays-the-name-game-with-ukraine-1409588947.

[9] Kiev International Institute of Sociology, viewed on 3 February 2015, http://www.kiis.com.ua/?lang=eng&cat=reports&id=236&page=1.

[10] Kamil Całus, 'Naddniestrze Formalizuje Prorosyjski Zwrot w Polityce Zagranicznej' ['Transnistria Formalises the Pro-Russian Turn in Foreign Affairs'], *OSW Analizy*, 28 November 2012, viewed on 15 August 2014, http://www.osw.waw.pl/pl/publikacje/analizy/2012-11-28/naddniestrze-formalizuje-prorosyjski-zwrot-w-polityce-zagranicznej All translations from Polish or Russian into English are mine.

[11] 'Евразийское Приднестровье' ['Eurasian Pridnestrovie'], viewed on 7 February 2015, http://eurasian.su/page/o-proekte.

[12] Kamil Całus, 'Naddniestrze wobec Perspektywy Aneksji przez Rosję' ['Transnistria Faced with the Prospect of Annexation by Russia'], *OSW Analizy*, 14 May 2014, viewed on 15 August 2014,

http://www.osw.waw.pl/pl/publikacje/analizy/2014-05-14/naddniestrze-wobec-perspektywy-aneksji-przez-rosje.

[13] Ibid.

[14] Информационное агентство *Ольвия-пресс* [Press agency *Ольвия-пресс*], viewed on 28 August 2014, http: //www.olvia.idknet.com/ol225-09-06.htm.

[15] Mykola Siruk, 'Why Is Vladimir Putin Losing Transnistria?' *day.kiev.ua* website, viewed on 3 September 2014, http://www.day.kiev.ua/en/article/topic-day/why-vladimir-putin-losing-transnistria.

[16] Gerard Toal and John O'Loughlin, 'How People in South Ossetia, Abkhazia and Transnistria Feel about Annexation by Russia,' viewed on 13 July 2014, http://www.washingtonpost.com/blogs/monkey-cage/wp/2014/03/20/how-people-in-south-ossetia-abkhazia-and-transnistria-feel-about-annexation-by-russia.

[17] IRI Baltic Surveys/The Gallup Organization, International Republic Institute, 'Public Opinion Survey: Residents of Moldova 7-27.06.2014,' viewed on 20 July 2014, http://www.iri.org/countries-and-programs/eurasia/moldova.

[18] CSCE Conflict Prevention Centre, 'The Transdniestrian Conflict in Moldova: Origins and Main Issues,' 1994, viewed on 18 August 2014, http://www.osce.org/moldova.

[19] The Constitution of the Republic of Moldova of 29.07.1994, viewed on 4 October 2014, http://www.constcourt.md/public/files/file/Actele%20Curtii/acte_en/MDA_Constitution_EN.pdf.

[20] Kamil Całus, 'Gagauzja: Rosnący Separatyzm w Mołdawii?' [Gagauzia: the Growing Separatism in Moldova'], *OSW Komentarze* 139 (2014): 1.

[21] Frank G. Hoffman, 'Hybrid vs. Compound War', *Armed Forces Journal* (2009), viewed on 14 January 2015, http://www.armedforcesjournal.com/hybrid-vs-compound-war.

[22] Russell W. Glenn, 'Thoughts on "Hybrid" Conflict,' *Small Wars Journal* (2009): 3, viewed on 14 January 2015, http://smallwarsjournal.com/jrnl/art/thoughts-on-hybrid-conflict.

[23] Oleg Shynkarenko, 'Russia's Hybrid War in Ukraine,' *Institute for War & Peace Reporting*, 2014, viewed on 20 January 2015, https://iwpr.net/global-voices/russias-hybrid-war-ukraine.

[24] David Alexander, 'Top NATO Commander Concerned About "Little Green Men" in Moldova,' *Atlantic Council* website, viewed on 20 January 2015, http://www.atlanticcouncil.org/blogs/natosource/top-nato-commander-concerned-about-little-green-men-in-moldova.

[25] Kamil Całus and Agata Wierzbowska-Miazga, 'Rosja nasila grę o Mołdawię' ['Russia Increases Its Game for Moldova'], *OSW Analizy*, 2 April 2014, viewed on 16 August 2014, http://www.osw.waw.pl/pl/publikacje/analizy/2014-04-02/rosja-nasila-gre-o-

moldawie.

[26] 'Association Agreement between the European Union and the European Atomic Energy Community and Their Member States, of the One Part, and the Republic of Moldova, of the Other Part', *European Union External Action*, 2014, viewed on 17 August 2014, http://eeas.europa.eu/moldova/assoagreement/assoagreement 2013_en.htm.

[27] EU Border Assistance Mission to Moldova and Ukraine, viewed on 17 August 2014, http://www.eubam.org.

[28] EUBAM, 'EUBAM's Area of Operations,' Annual Report 2013, viewed on 15 January 2015, http://www.eubam.org/en/knowledge/eubam_pubs/ar_2013.

[29] Matthew Rojansky, *Prospects for Unfreezing Moldova's Frozen Conflict in Transnistria* (Washington: U.S. Commission on Security and Cooperation in Europe, 2011), 3.

[30] Kamil Całus, 'Mołdawski Sąd Konstytucyjny Uznał Język Rumuński za Państwowy' ['The Moldavian Constitutional Court Recognized the Romanian Language As an Official Language'], *OSW Analizy*, 11 December 2013, viewed on 16 August 2014,
http://www.osw.waw.pl/pl/publikacje/analizy/2013-12-11/moldawski-sad-konstytucyjny-uznal-jezyk-rumunski-za-panstwowy.

[31] IRI Baltic Surveys/The Gallup Organization, 'Moldova National Voter Study,' August 20 - September 2, 2011, *Mediafax.ro* website, viewed on 15 January 2015, http://www.iri.org/sites/default/files/2011%20June%206%20Survey%20of%20Moldova%20Public%20Opinion,%20January%2024-February%207,%202011.pdf.

[32] Andrzej Wierzbicki, 'Elita Władzy wobec Problemów Narodowościowych i Konfesyjnych,' ['Political Elites Towards Ethnic and Confessional Issues'] in *Przywództwo i Elity Polityczne w Krajach WNP* , ed. Tadeusz Bodio and Wojciech Jakubowski (Warszawa: Oficyna Wydawnicza ASPRA-JR, 2011), 161-164.

[33] Alexander Dugin, 'The Eurasian Idea,' 2004, viewed on 20 June 2014, http://evrazia.org/modules.php?name=News&file=article&sid=1886.

[34] Alicja Curanović, 'Elity Władzy Krajów WNP wobec Rosyjskiej Koncepcji Cywilizacji Eurazjatyckiej,' ['Political Elites of CIS Countries Towards the Russian Concept of Eurasian Civilization'] in *Przywództwo i Elity Polityczne w Krajach WNP*, ed. Tadeusz Bodio and Wojciech Jakubowski (Warszawa: Oficyna Wydawnicza ASPRA-JR, 2011), 381-382.

[35] Marek Menkiszak, 'Doktryna Putina: Tworzenie Koncepcyjnych Podstaw Rosyjskiej Dominacji na Obszarze Postradzieckim' ['Putin's Doctrine: Conceptual Basis for Russian Domination in the Post-Soviet Area'], *OSW Komentarze* 131 (2014): 2.

[36] Alina Cherata, in this volume.

[37] 'Address by President of the Russian Federation.'

[38] Menkiszak, 'Doktryna Putina,' 4-5.

[39] 'Address by President of the Russian Federation.'

[40] Rojansky, *Prospects for Unfreezing*, 2.

[41] Witold Rodkiewicz, ed., *Transnistrian Conflict after 20 Years* (Warsaw, Chisinau: Centre for Eastern Studies, Institute for Development and Social Initiatives Viitorul, 2011), 6.

[42] '"Меморандум Козака": Российский план объединения Молдовы и Приднестровья' ['Kozak Memorandum': The Russian Plan for the Unification of Moldova and Transnistria'] viewed on 20 August 2014, http://www.regnum.ru/news/458547.html.

[43] Eurasian Economic Commission, 'Eurasian Economic Integration. Facts and Figures,' 2013, viewed on 12 June 2014, http://eurasiancommission.org/ru/Documents.

[44] Community for Democracy and Rights of Nations, viewed on 4 October 2014, http://www.community-dpr.org/about/index.php.html.

[45] Marcin Kosienkowski, 'Wspólnota na rzecz Demokracji i Praw Narodów-Geneza, Ustrój i Funkcjonowanie,' ['Community for Democracy and Rights of Nations: Origin, Structure and Functioning'] in *Wspólnota Niepodległych Państw: Fragmentacja – Bezpieczeństwo - Konflikty etniczne*, ed. Tomasz Kapuśniak (Lublin-Warszawa: Instytut Europy Środkowo-Wschodniej, Wydawnictwo KUL, 2011), 89.

[46] Katarzyna Czerewacz-Filipowicz, in this volume

[47] Статистический Ежегодник 2014, Государственная Служба Статистики Приднестровской Молдавской Республики, Тирасполь 2014. Statistical Yearbook 2014, The National Statistical Service of the Pridnestrovian Moldavian Republic, Tiraspol 2014.

[48] Aleksandra Jarosiewicz and Ewa Fischer, 'Eurazjatycka Unia Gospodarcza–więcej Polityki, mniej Gospodarki' ['Eurasian Economic Union – More Politics, Less Economy'], *OSW Komentarze*,157 (2015): 2.

[49] Kamil Całus, 'Rosyjskie Sankcje wobec Mołdawii. Niewielkie Efekty, Spory Potencjał' ['Russian Sanctions towards Moldova: Small Effects, Great Potential'], *OSW Komentarze* 152 (2014): 1-6.

[50] Nicu Popescu and Leonid Litra, 'Transnistria: A Bottom-up Solution,' *European Council on Foreign Relations, Policy Brief* 63 (2012): 2.

[51] Ibid., 5.

[52] Kamil Całus, 'Problemy finansowe Naddniestrza' ['Financial Problems of Transnistria'], *OSW Analizy*, 9 July 2014, viewed on 15 August 2014, http://www.osw.waw.pl/pl/publikacje/analizy/2014-07-09/problemy-finansowe-naddniestrza.

[53] National Bureau of Statistics of the Republic of Moldova, viewed on 5 February 2015, http://statbank.statistica.md/pxweb/Dialog/Saveshow.asp.

[54] Kamil Całus, 'Russia's Embargo on Moldovan Goods Is Extended,' *OSW Analizy*, 23 July 2014, viewed on 16 August 2014, http://www.osw.waw.pl/en/publikacje/analyses/2014-07-23/russias-embargo-moldovan-goods-extended.
[55] Ministry of Foreign Affairs of Pridnestrovian Moldavian Republic, 'Threat to Peace on the Dniester,' viewed on 2 February 2015, http://mfa-pmr.org/en/mxP.
[56] Organization for Security and Co-operation in Europe, viewed on 18 August 2014, http://www.osce.org/cio/119489.
[57] Paul Ivan, 'Transnistria-Where to?' *European Policy Centre, Policy Brief* 13 (2014): 1.
[58] 'Meseberg Memorandum,' 4-5 June 2010, viewed on 26 November 2014, http://www.russianmission.eu/sites/default/files/user/files/2010-06-05-meseberg-memorandum.pdf.
[59] Popescu and Litra, 'Transnistria: A Bottom-up Solution', 8.
[60] Conference on Confidence Building Measures on the Transdniestria Conflict Settlement Process, Germany, 2014, viewed on 12 August 2014, http://www.osce.org/moldova/120255?download=true.

Bibliography

'Address by President of the Russian Federation'. *The Kremlin* website. 18 March 2014. Viewed on 26 June 2014. http://eng.kremlin.ru/transcripts/6889.

Alexander, David. 'Top NATO Commander Concerned about "Little Green Men" in Moldova.' Atlantic Council website. 2014. Viewed on 20 January 2015. http://www.atlanticcouncil.org/blogs/natosource/top-nato-commander-concerned-about-little-green-men-in-moldova.

'Association Agreement between the European Union and the European Atomic Energy Community and Their Member States, of the One Part, and the Republic of Moldova, of the Other Part'. European Union External Action, 2014. Viewed on 17 August 2014. http://eeas.europa.eu/moldova/assoagreement/assoagreement-2013_en.htm.

Brzeziński, Zbigniew. 'The Premature Partnership.' *Foreign Affairs* 73/2 (1994): 67-82.

Całus, Kamil. 'Gagauzja: Rosnący Separatyzm w Mołdawii?' *OSW Komentarze* 139 (2014): 1-9.

————. 'Mołdawski Sąd Konstytucyjny Uznał Język Rumuński za Państwowy,' *OSW Analizy*, 11 December 2013. Viewed on 16 August 2014. http://www.osw.waw.pl/pl/publikacje/analizy/2013-12-11/moldawski-sad-konstytucyjny-uznal-jezyk-rumunski-za-panstwowy.

————. 'Naddniestrze Formalizuje Prorosyjski Zwrot w Polityce Zagranicznej,' *OSW Analizy*, 28 November 2012. Viewed on 15 August 2014. http://www.osw.waw.pl/pl/publikacje/analizy/2012-11-28/naddniestrze-formalizuje-prorosyjski-zwrot-w-polityce-zagranicznej.

————. 'Naddniestrze wobec Perspektywy Aneksji przez Rosję', *OSW Analizy*, 14 May 2014. Viewed 15 August 2014. http://www.osw.waw.pl/pl/publikacje/analizy/2014-05-14/naddniestrze-wobec-perspektywy-aneksji-przez-rosje.

————. 'Problemy Finansowe Naddniestrza,' *OSW Analizy*, 9 July 2014. Viewed on 15 August 2014. http://www.osw.waw.pl/pl/publikacje/analizy/2014-07-09/problemy-finansowe-naddniestrza.

————. 'Rosyjskie Sankcje wobec Mołdawii. Niewielkie Efekty, Spory Potencjał.' *OSW Komentarze* 152 (2014): 1-6.

————. 'Russia's Embargo on Moldovan Goods is Extended,' *OSW Analizy*, 23 July 2014. Viewed on 16 August 2014. http://www.osw.waw.pl/en/publikacje/analyses/2014-07-23/russias-embargo-moldovan-goods-extended.

Całus, Kamil and Agata Wierzbowska-Miazga. 'Rosja Nasila Grę o Mołdawię,' *OSW Analizy*, 2 April 2014. Viewed on 16 August 2014. http://www.osw.waw.pl/pl/publikacje/analizy/2014-04-02/rosja-nasila-gre-o-moldawie.

Community for Democracy and Rights of Nations. Viewed on 4 October 2014. http://www.community-dpr.org/about/index.php.html.

Conference on Confidence Building Measures on the Transdniestria Conflict Settlement Process. Germany, 2014. Viewed on 12 August 2014. http://www.osce.org/moldova/120255?download=true.

CSCE Conflict Prevention Centre. 'The Transdniestrian Conflict in Moldova: Origins and Main Issues,' 1994. Viewed on 18 August 2014. http://www.osce.org/moldova.

Curanovič, Alicja. 'Elity Władzy Krajów WNP wobec Rosyjskiej Koncepcji Cywilizacji Eurazjatyckiej.' In *Przywództwo i Elity Polityczne w Krajach WNP T. 2*, edited by Tadeusz Bodio and Wojciech Jakubowski, 381-382. Warszawa: Oficyna Wydawnicza ASPRA-JR, 2011.

Dugin, Alexander. 'The Eurasian Idea', International Eurasian Movement, 2014. Viewed on 20 June 2014. http://evrazia.org/modules.php?name=News&file=article&sid=1886).

'Евразийское Приднестровье' ['Eurasian Pridnestrovie']. Viewed on 7 February 2015. http://eurasian.su/page/o-proekte.

EU Border Assistance Mission to Moldova and Ukraine. Viewed on 17 August 2014. http://www.eubam.org.

EUBAM. 'EUBAM's Area of Operations.' Annual Report 2013. Viewed on 15 January 2015. http://www.eubam.org/en/knowledge/eubam_pubs/ar_2013.

Eurasian Economic Commission. 'Eurasian Economic Integration. Facts and Figures,' 2013. Viewed on 12 June 2014. http://eurasiancommission.org/ru/Documents.

Freedom House. 'Freedom in the World 2013. Transnistria.' Viewed on 15 August 2014. http://www.freedomhouse.org/report/freedom-world/2013/transnistria#.U85SoL F9bKE.

Glenn, Russell W. 'Thoughts on "Hybrid" Conflict.' *Small Wars Journal* (2009): 3. Viewed on 14 January 2015. http://smallwarsjournal.com/jrnl/art/thoughts-on-hybrid-conflict.

Hoffman, Frank G. 'Hybrid vs. Compound War.' *Armed Forces Journal*, 1 October 2009. Viewed on 14 January 2015. http://www.armedforcesjournal.com/hybrid-vs-compound-war.

International Court of Justice. 'Accordance with International Law of the Unilateral Declaration of Independence in Respect of Kosovo (Request for Advisory Opinion).' Viewed on 19 June 2014. http://www.icj-cij.org/docket/index.php?p1=3&p2=4&k=21&case=141&code=kos&p3=4

IRI Baltic Surveys/The Gallup Organization. 'Moldova National Voter Study,' August 20 - September 2, 2011, *Mediafax.ro* website. Viewed on 15 January 2015. http://www.iri.org/sites/default/files/2011%20June%206%20Survey%20of%20Moldova%20Public%20Opinion,%20January%2024-February%207,%202011.pdf.

IRI Baltic Surveys/The Gallup Organization, International Republic Institute. 'Public Opinion Survey. Residents of Moldova 7-27.06.2014.' Viewed on 20 July 2014. http://www.iri.org/countries-and-programs/eurasia/moldova.

Ivan, Paul. 'Transnistria-Where To?' *European Policy Centre, Policy Brief* 13 (2014): 1-4.

Jarosiewicz, Aleksandra and Ewa Fischer. 'Eurazjatycka Unia Gospodarcza–więcej Polityki, mniej Gospodarki.' *OSW Komentarze* 157 (2015): 1-7.

Kiev International Institute of Sociology. Viewed on 3 February 2015. http://www.kiis.com.ua/?lang=eng&cat=reports&id=236&page=1.

Kosienkowski, Marcin. 'Wspólnota na rzecz Demokracji i Praw Narodów - Geneza, Ustrój i Funkcjonowanie.' In *Wspólnota Niepodległych Państw: Fragmentacja – Bezpieczeństwo - Konflikty Etniczne*, edited by Tomasz Kapuśniak, 87-115. Lublin-Warszawa: Instytut Europy Środkowo-Wschodniej, Wydawnictwo KUL, 2011.

'Меморандум Козака': Российский план объединения Молдовы и Приднестровья'. Viewed 20 August 2014, http://www.regnum.ru/news/458547.html.

Menkiszak, Marek. 'Doktryna Putina: Tworzenie koncepcyjnych podstaw rosyjskiej dominacji na obszarze postradzieckim.' *OSW Komentarze* 131 (2014): 2-12.

'Meseberg Memorandum,' 4-5 June 2010. Viewed on 26 November 2014. http://www.russianmission.eu/sites/default/files/user/files/2010-06-05-meseberg-memorandum.pdf.

Ministry of Foreign Affairs of Pridnestrovian Moldavian Republic. Viewed on 2 February 2015. http://mfa-pmr.org/en.

National Bureau of Statistics of the Republic of Moldova. Viewed on 5 February 2015. http://statbank.statistica.md/pxweb/Dialog/Saveshow.asp.

Organization for Security and Co-operation in Europe. Viewed on 18 August 2014. http://www.osce.org/cio/119489.

Popescu, Nicu, and Leonid Litra, 'Transnistria: a Bottom-up Solution.' *European Council on Foreign Relations, Policy Brief* 63 (2012): 1-16.

Rodkiewicz, Witold, ed. *Transnistrian Conflict after 20 Years.* Warsaw, Chisinau: Centre for Eastern Studies, Institute for Development and Social Initiatives Viitorul, 2011.

Rojansky, Matthew. *Prospects for Unfreezing Moldova's Frozen Conflict in Transnistria.* Washington: U.S. Commission on Security and Cooperation in Europe, 2011.

Shynkarenko, Oleg. 'Russia's Hybrid War in Ukraine.' Institute for War & Peace Reporting, 2014. Viewed on 20 January 2015. https://iwpr.net/global-voices/russias-hybrid-war-ukraine.

Siruk, Mykola. 'Why is Vladimir Putin Losing Transnistria?' *day.kiev.ua* website. Viewed on 3 September 2014. http://www.day.kiev.ua/en/article/topic-day/why-vladimir-putin-losing-transnistria.

Sonne, Paul. 'With *Novorossiya* Putin Plays the Name Game with Ukraine.' *The Wall Street Journal* 2014. Viewed on 17 January 2015. http://www.wsj.com/articles/with-novorossiya-putin-plays-the-name-game-with-ukraine-1409588947.

Tames, Ismee. 'Expecting War in Europe: Fears and Anxieties about War.' In *Fears and Anxieties in the 21st Century: The European Context and Beyond*, edited by Catalin Ghita and Robert Beshara. *Oxford: Inter-Disciplinary Press*, 2015.

Toal, Gerard, and John O'Loughlin. 'How People in South Ossetia, Abkhazia and Transnistria Feel about Annexation by Russia.' Viewed on 13 July 2014. http://www.washingtonpost.com/blogs/monkey-cage/wp/2014/03/20/how-people-in-south-ossetia-abkhazia-and-transnistria-feel-about-annexation-by-russia.

The Constitution of the Republic of Moldova of 29.07.1994. Constitutional Court of Moldova. Viewed on 4 October 2014. http://www.constcourt.md/public/files/file/Actele%20Curtii/acte_en/MDA_Constitution_EN.pdf.

'Transnistria's Appeal for Recognition to United Nations is Illogical,' *Moldova.org* website. Viewed on 2 September 2014. http://www.moldova.org/transnistrias-appeal-for-recognition-to-united-nations-is-illogical-211282-eng.

Wierzbicki, Andrzej. 'Elita Władzy wobec Problemów Narodowościowych i Konfesyjnych.' In *Przywództwo i Elity Polityczne w Krajach WNP* T. 2, edited by Tadeusz Bodio and Wojciech Jakubowski, 161-164. Warszawa: Oficyna Wydawnicza ASPRA-JR, 2011.

Agnieszka Konopelko, doctor of political science, works at Bialystok University of Technology, Faculty of Management. Her research interests concentrate on transformation processes on the post-Soviet area and its relations with the EU.

Fears and Anxieties Resulting in Regional Integration in the Post-Soviet Area

Katarzyna Czerewacz-Filipowicz

Abstract

Searching for the path of economic development as well as political stability and security are the factors making post-Soviet states lean towards participation in a variety of regional integration agreements. Regional Integration Agreements (RIAs) are a positive phenomenon being set up mainly to make the economic development of the member states more dynamic. However, it seems interesting to look at the various integration groups in the post-Soviet area through the prism of fears and anxieties inducing the states to participate in them. Since the collapse of the USSR in 1991, the newly established countries were accompanied by concerns for the future. Twelve of them decided to join the Commonwealth of Independent States in fear of the consequences of the loss of the previously-functioning political and economic ties. Further initiatives emerging in the region can also be analysed from the perspective of types of concerns the Member States were driven by. The first group of reasons can be economic concerns related to: dependence on preferential prices for Russian energy resources, the lack of a basis for economic development, the fear of economic crises caused by ineffective management and the need for help from the Russian Federation and dependence on the Russian pipelines. The second group of reasons is the fear related to the safety and security of borders. In a situation of economic and political crisis many countries fear a lack of support from Russia. On the one hand, Russia takes many integration steps from fear of losing international position and its influence in the region. On the other hand, the fear of Russia (of the Russian sanctions and Russian military power) for some countries of the region is an element determining the cooperation with this country. However, for the others it is the cause for creating groups competing against Russia.

Key Words: Regional Integration Agreements, Russian Federation, the CIS, the Eurasian Economic Community.

*****

1. Introduction: Theoretical Background

International regional integration can be caused by a variety of fears and anxieties. It can be a remedy for them. On the other hand, it may incite fears and anxieties in the post-Soviet area or in other parts of the world. The main aim of this chapter is to present fears and anxieties on the territory of the post-Soviet countries (former USSR - The Union of Soviet Socialist Republics) from the perspective of international regional integration processes.

After the collapse of the USSR fifteen new countries were created: Armenia, Azerbaijan, Belarus, Estonia, Georgia, Kazakhstan, Kyrgyzstan, Latvia, Lithuania, Moldova, Russia, Tajikistan, Turkmenistan, Ukraine, Uzbekistan. They are called 'post-Soviet countries.' In this chapter, the term 'post-Soviet' refers mainly to twelve of them: Armenia, Azerbaijan, Belarus, Georgia, Kazakhstan, Kyrgyzstan, Moldova, Russia, Tajikistan, Turkmenistan, Ukraine, Uzbekistan because Estonia, Latvia, Lithuania joined the European Union on 1 May 2014 and have never participated in the RIAs in the post-Soviet space.

It is not only in the analysed part of the world that international regional economic integration is treated as a remedy for concerns regarding economic development. For example, The Economic Commission for Latin America in their report entitled: 'The Latin American Common Market and the Multilateral Payments System,' concludes that 'the common market [and generally regional economic integration] should offer each and all of the Latin American countries equal opportunities of expending their economic growth.'[1]

Moreover, as evidenced by Ernst B. Haas, political international integration 'would contribute to world peace by creating ever-expanding islands of practical cooperation, eventually spilling over into the controversy-laden fields which threaten us directly with (...) destruction.'[2] In the context of countering different fears and anxieties, Bela Balassa define regional integration as 'a process (...) which encompasses various measures abolishing discrimination between economic units belonging to different national states ... .'[3]

After the collapse of the USSR, the newly created states had to define their role and place in both the region and the world. Politics of regional integration in many cases was an attempt to determine the path of economic and political development, (e.g. accession to the European Union of Lithuania, Latvia and Estonia, the close connection between the Republic of Belarus and the Russian Federation).

The integration of the post-Soviet area is considered in both political and economic sciences.

Some researchers emphasize that it is 'holding-together regionalism': the integration of countries which, until recently, were parts of a single political entity.[4] In Libman's and Vinokurov's study, it should be noted that integration is really about stopping disintegration and maintaining former economic ties. By contrast, sceptics treat the integration initiatives in the post-Soviet area as a transitional political concept without a future.[5]

There are also researchers taking a different perspective by which the integration of the post-Soviet area is only a part of Russia's policy of multilateralism, and creating a multipolar world.[6] On the other hand, it has been more and more often emphasized that the purpose of integration in this case is not simply to bring the member states close together in terms of economy, but, rather, to influence their economic development in a positive way.[7]

From a theoretical point of view, the processes of regional economic integration are the amalgamation of separate economies into larger free trading regions.[8] In this way, regional economic integration is known as a very positive phenomenon in the contemporary world's economy, the phenomenon being set up mainly to make the economic development of member states more dynamic. Countries joining regional groups expect faster economic growth, better position in the international division of labour, strengthening their position on the international scene.

This chapter presents different approaches to the problem of regional integration, connected with fears and anxieties in the post-Soviet area with special consideration to the economic ones.

After the collapse of the USSR, many different regional integration concepts came into being. The largest and probably still the most famous one is the Commonwealth of Independent States (the CIS) to which most post-Soviet countries still belong (Armenia, Azerbaijan, Belarus, Kazakhstan, Kyrgyzstan, Russia, Tajikistan, Uzbekistan, Turkmenistan is an observer and Ukraine is still officially linked with CIS). Unfortunately, this organization is also very inefficient. Many expectations and agreements did not provide any results. This is why many other smaller organizations were created like: the Common State of Russia and Belarus, the Common Economic Space, the Organisation of Central Asian Cooperation, the Collective Security Treaty Organization, the Shanghai Cooperation Organization, the GUAM Organization for Democracy and Economic Development, the Eurasian Economic Community (the EurAsEC covered Russia, Belarus, Kazakhstan, Kyrgyzstan, Tajikistan), the Eurasian Economic Union and many others.

The most promising initiative is today's Eurasian Economic Union. This organization has its origin in the Eurasian Economic Community created in 2000. The part of the EurAsEC transformed into the Customs Union in 2010 first and then into the Single Economic Space in 2012. In particular, the Eurasian Economic Union has incited many fears and anxieties. The EEU was established during the current armed conflict in Ukraine constituting a real threat to the security of the entire region. (The Eurasian Economic Union was also established during the European Union and US economic sanctions affecting Russia and other members of the organization, and the Russian Federation sanctions directed against the European Union and the USA) Ismee Tames notes that the conflict in Ukraine may result in another world war.[9]

Surprising, and partly dictated by fear, is also the current composition of membership of the Eurasian Economic Union. Besides the states forming the Customs Union: Russia, Belarus and Kazakhstan, there are also Kyrgyzstan and Armenia. Armenia's membership seems particularly surprising because it signed an agreement with the European Union entitled 'The Deep and Comprehensive

Free Trade Area' (DCFTA) and then changed the direction of its foreign policy and joined the EEU.

The main question is: Why are the countries that used to be united under the USSR and that decided in 1991 to dissolve the said union keep looking for the possibility of integration? There are many answers to this question and some of them are connected with fears and anxieties nurtured by people who live in post-Soviet area.

2. Different Fears and Anxieties in the Post-Soviet Area

Fears and anxieties connected with economic development and political stability and security are factors making the post-Soviet states lean towards participation in a variety of regional integration agreements both inside and outside this region.

A big group of reasons is the fear related to the safety and security of borders that motivated Kyrgyzstan, Tajikistan, Kazakhstan and Uzbekistan to join the Shanghai Cooperation Organization. The region of Central Asia (including Kazakhstan, Kyrgyzstan, Tajikistan, Turkmenistan and Uzbekistan) is characterized by ethnic and cultural diversity resulting in many tensions and conflicts. One of serious dangers is Islamic fundamentalism, among others, there are questions regarding protection of boundaries.[10]

Agnieszka Konopelko, in her chapter entitled 'The Case of Transnistria in the Context of the Russian Eurasian Union Project,' presents fears and anxieties related to ethnic conflicts, separatism and, in consequence, disintegration of the territories of the particular states of the post-Soviet area, she then collates them with 'Putin's doctrine of foreign and security policy. The doctrine emphasizes not only reintegration of the post-Soviet area but also restoration of the unity of the "Russian-speaking community".'[11] In the context of her work two more regional integration links with fears and anxieties can be drawn. From the perspective of some countries (including Russia) international regional integration can be a remedy for fear of disintegration of the national territory. On the other hand, from the perspective of other countries (examples indicated by Agnieszka Konopelko) regional integration processes initiated by the Russian Federation can contribute to disintegration of their territory.[12]

On the one hand, the Russian Federation takes many integration steps for fear of both losing its international position and influence in the region. The Russian people still have in their minds the period of the early 1990s when their country lost the position of a super power on the international stage. Neither the last president of the USSR Mikhail Gorbachev nor the first president of the Russian Federation Boris Yeltsin were prepared to cope with economic and political problems. These presidencies and connected with them Russian foreign policies in the early 1990s refer to a period which the Russians call 'Russia's internal withdrawal' meaning the necessity to concentrate on internal problems.[13] The

Russian politicians at that time saw closer relations with the West as an opportunity to regain the status of a super power. This unfortunate foreign policy failed as it did not establish the required structures and systems of relations in the territory of Eurasia. There also appeared a view of '*the end of Eurasia*' being in this sense a synonym for the Russian Empire.[14] When Vladimir Putin took the position of the President of the Russian Federation the Russian domestic and foreign policies changed considerably. He enforced the idea of strengthening Russia's position in the post-Soviet space as a fundament of building a new power status of his country. Such a policy has been accepted by the majority of the Russian society and still seems to be a good remedy for fears and anxieties connected with the position of Russia on the international scene.

On the other hand, for some countries of the region fear of Russia, such as of sanctions and Russian military power, is an element determining the cooperation with the Russian Federation as part of the Eurasian Economic Union (former the EurAsEC) or the Commonwealth of Independent States (including the CIS Free Trade Agreement). However, for others, it has become the cause for creating groups competing against Russia (e.g. the GUAM Organization for Democracy and Economic Development and the Economic Cooperation Organization).

A completely different group of reasons are related to economic concerns:

- Dependence on preferential prices for Russian energy resources (e.g. Belarus in the EurAsEC or the Customs Union),
- The fear of economic crises caused by ineffective management and the need for help from the Russian Federation (e.g. Kyrgyzstan, Tajikistan) – many of these countries are very vulnerable to economic crises because of their weaker economies and also because of their dependence on the prices of raw materials and agricultural products,
- Dependence on the Russian pipelines (e.g. Kazakhstan in the EurAsEC, the Customs Union, the Eurasian Economic Union). Kazakhstan possesses huge resources of gas, oil, uranium but still a big part of transit of those materials goes through the Russian territory,
- The lack of the grounds for economic development (e.g Kyrgyzstan in the EurAsEC). Within the post-Soviet territory there are some of poor countries and even some of the poorest countries in the contemporary world's economy,
- Social and socioeconomic fears and anxieties are connected either low standard of living and unemployment (e.g. Tajikistan, Ukraine), or low birth-rate (e.g. the Russian

Federation). These problems have caused migrations which determine other fears and anxieties.

- Fear of Chinese economic expansion. Today, China is the most important economic partner for almost all Central Asian countries (see Table 1), but the growth of China's position, as a trade investment partner and a source of capital, is so fast, that it makes those countries afraid about their future economic independence. In this case, the integration between the Russian Federation and the post-Soviet region is a kind of alternative based on economic diversification of foreign relations.

Table 1: Main trade partners of the Central Asia countries

Kazakhstan Trade					
Export			Import		
No.	Partner	%	No.	Partner	%
1.	China	23.45	1.	China	31.11
2.	France	9.99	2.	Russia	20.79
3.	Russia	8.30	3.	Germany	6.34
Kyrgyzstan Trade					
Export			Import		
No.	Partner	%	No.	Partner	%
1.	Kazakhstan	28.07	1.	China	51.71
2.	Uzbekistan	27.92	2.	Russia	21.16
3.	Russia	11.10	3.	Kazakhstan	7.79
Tajikistan Trade					
Export			Import		
No.	Partner	%	No.	Partner	%
1.	Turkey	29.79	1.	China	41.61
2.	China	9.38	2.	Russia	15.90
3.	Iran	7.26	3.	Kazakhstan	12.57
Turkmenistan Trade					
Export			Import		
No.	Partner	%	No.	Partner	%
1.	China	69.47	1.	Turkey	22.75
2.	Italy	4.66	2.	Russia	15.53
3.	United Arab Emirates	3.13	3.	China	13.27
Uzbekistan Trade					
Export			Import		
No.	Partner	%	No.	Partner	%
1.	China	28.14	1.	China	20.58
2.	Russia	19.41	2.	Russia	20.04
3.	Kazakhstan	12.62	3.	South Korea	15.50

Source: Own calculation on the base of Quarterly 03/2014, Quarterly 06/2014, Direction Of Trade Statistics, International Monetary Fund, Washington 2014.

3. Economic Fears as a Factor Determining Regional Integration

Within the territory of the post-Soviet region, there are many particularly poor countries which need some driving factors for their economies. On the one hand, participation in regional integration agreements help them get these driving factors. On the other hand, wrong decisions can perpetuate their economic backwardness.

Table 2: Main economic factors of post-Soviet countries in 2013

Country	Area (thousands km²)	Population (thousands persons)	GDP (billion USD)	GDP per capita (USD)
Azerbaijan	86.60	9 122	73.54	7899.60
Armenia	29.80	3 332	10.55	3208.31
Belarus	207.60	9 434	71.71	7577.08
Georgia	69.70	4 469	16.16	3604.51
Kazakhstan	2724.90	16 674	220.35	12843.21
Kyrgyzstan	199.90	5 532	7.23	1280.17
Moldova	33.80	3 557	7.94	2229.19
Russia	17098.20	142 411	2118.01	14818.64
Tajikistan	142.60	7 801	8.50	1044.95
Turkmenistan	488.10	5 526	40.57	7112.00
Ukraine	603.70	45 598	177.83	3919.41
Uzbekistan	447.40	29 100	56.48	1867.54

Source: International Monetary Fund, World Economic Outlook Database, April 2014.

Armenia's GDP per capita is a little more than 3000 USD, Moldova's GDP per capita is a little more than 2000 GDP, Uzbekistan's – below 2000 USD and Kyrgyzstan's and Tajikistan's GDPs per capita are a little more than 1000 USD. It means that, in these countries, about 20% (to even 30% in Tajikistan) of the population live for less than 1.25 USD per day.

Some reasons for this situation are connected with a legacy from the USSR, but many of them are connected with changes in the contemporary world's economy, globalization, geopolicy and geoeconomy of particular countries and the very fast development of some neighbouring countries.

The Central Asian countries (including Kazakhstan, Kyrgyzstan, Tajikistan, Turkmenistan and Uzbekistan) are of interest to many countries (China, Russia, Turkey, Islamic countries, the US, and to some degree the European Union), because of their geostrategic location, and because of their enormous resources of crude oil, natural gas and uranium. They are also a good market for Chinese and Russian products. The Central Asian countries, being often very poor countries are looking for the possibility of a stable economic growth and lower economic dependency on strong neighbours.

The Central Asian countries are closely linked to both Russia and China – though in different areas. The Central Asian countries are strongly dependent on the Russian labour market. Almost half of Tajikistan and Kyrgyzstan GDP comes from remittances received by Tajik's or Kyrgyz's workers in Russia. On the other hand, this money earned in Russia is spent on Chinese products. China is the largest trade partner for Kyrgyzstan, Kazakhstan and Tajikistan and Chinese expansion has been growing, so paradoxically the regional integration within the post-Soviet region can be a way of diversification of economic connections of these countries. Even Kazakhstan, big and rich in raw materials, decided to enter partnership with Russia as counterbalance to Chinese economic dependency.

A completely different and intriguing is the Russian trade position on the post-Soviet and the global market. Since the collapse of the USSR, the Russian Federation, to a much higher degree than other post-Soviet countries, has diversified the direction of its trade. Today (see Table 3), the most important trading partners of Russia are the European Union countries with the 50% share in Russian turnover. While the current position of the Commonwealth of Independent States countries is about 9%, with the share of Belarus amounting to 4.6% and Kazakhstan's share is 3%.

Table 3: Main trade partners of the Russian Federation in 2013

Export			Import		
No.	Partner	%	No.	Partner	%
	World	100.00		World	100.00
1.	Netherlands	10.77	1.	China	16.60
2.	Germany	8.25	2.	Germany	12.58
3.	China	6.85	3.	Ukraine	4.87
	EU	52.90		EU	41.90
	CIS	10.20		CIS	9.50

Source: Own calculation on the base of: Quarterly 03/2014, Quarterly 06/2014, Direction Of Trade Statistics, International Monetary Fund, Washington 2014.

This is a unique situation because Russia has integrated with the countries which are currently not its main trading partners. So the question is why Russia wants to integrate at the economic plane with the post-Soviet countries. The main reason for the direction of the integration processes created by Russia are probably caused by the Russian turnover with particular countries and structures.

Almost 80% of the Russian exports to the European Union countries are mineral fuels, lubricants and related materials, whereas the Russian imports from the European Union are dominated by highly processed goods, such as: machinery and transport equipment (almost 50%), chemicals and related products (nearly 20%), and miscellaneous manufactured articles (more than 10%).[15]

These relations are, to a very high degree, of intersectional nature. Russia has been afraid of being only a raw material exporter. Oil and gas are strategic products but one day they can be replaced by other sources of energy. So a supplier of raw materials can be easily replaced by another supplier and can also be eliminated by the latest technology.

This situation is a kind of a challenge and does not seem to be in accordance with the Russian Federation's vision of economic development and the Russian vision of the world's order. According to an official Russian strategy, the Russian President would like to see Russia as an economy based on knowledge, specializing in the latest technologies and, most of all, a superpower.

The recipients of the highly processed products are and may be in the future the Commonwealth of Independent States members (especially countries of the Eurasian Economic Union). On the one hand, Russian relations with the CIS countries are intrasectional in many sectors, e.g., in the field of machinery and transport equipment, chemicals and related products as well as metals, and, more importantly – fuels. On the other hand, Russian products are very competitive in the CIS countries, including highly processed products and therefore the markets of the Commonwealth of Independent States get a lot of different Russian innovations related to the machinery and equipment industry, transport industry, information technology, telecommunications, aerospace or arms.

Some other economic fears in the post-Soviet area are connected with the position of these countries in the international division of labour resulting in their vulnerability to economic crises. For this reason, paradoxically, periods of economic downturn result in strengthening the integration processes in the post-Soviet region. Most CIS countries fearing economic collapse decide to look for help through closer cooperation with Russia. In turn, the Russian Federation has been using periods of downturn to increase its influence in the region. A good example is the crisis of 2008-2011.

Economic crises are an extreme danger to the poorest post-Soviet countries, not only because of economic consequences, but also because they can threaten the stability of these countries, the integrity of their territories and generally their statehood. A good illustration of this mechanism is Kyrgyzstan during the international crisis of 2009-2010. The global economic crisis that hit Kyrgyzstan in 2009 was additionally deepened by a political crisis in the country. The events of April and June 2010 led the country to political instability and economic depression. It had serious consequences in many sectors:

- unemployment, already high in this country, grew even more,
- about three thousand residential buildings and more than three hundred public buildings were damaged,
- many companies suffered losses,

- the closure of the borders with neighbouring countries, almost led to the suspension of exports of agricultural production and caused considerable damage to enterprises of the light and food-processing industry.

Economic and political events also resulted in a decrease of investment attractiveness of the Kyrgyz Republic as well a significant deterioration in the standard of living of its citizens. International assistance, given mainly by the Russian Federation (delivered through various channels such as the Anti-Crisis Fund of the Eurasian Economic Community), was the only solution to the Kyrgyz problems.

Despite its own economic problems Russia has taken a number of actions to increase its influence in the countries of the former Eurasian Economic Community, which has been affected by the crisis to an even greater extent. In exchange for economic and political concessions, Russia provided Belarus, Kyrgyzstan and Tajikistan with stabilization loans and investments. This created a favourable situation for Russian companies which could cheaply acquire assets in those countries. Belarus agreed to create a joint air defence system, and Kyrgyzstan decided to close the American base in Manas near Bishkek.

4. Social and Socioeconomic Fears Influencing the International Integration

International migration is a result of uneven allocation of factors of production across the modern world. This situation stems from disparities in economic development. It is then not surprising that the dynamic development of various forms of international regional integration creates favourable conditions for international migration. This phenomenon has become an inherent part of RIAs's (Regional Integration Agreements) progress. It does not, however, change the fact that migration triggers many fears and anxieties both in the country of immigration and emigration. In the context of the European Union this problem is taken up in a chapter entitled 'Invasion and Tidal Waves: Fictionalising EU Migration' by Stefania Alina Cherata.[16]

The collapse of the Soviet Union resulted in migration between the former Soviet republics gaining international status. This required a new approach to regulating migration processes. The issue additionally hindering the situation became economic disparities between the post-Soviet states that had just come into existence (see Table 2). They arose due to not being equally supplied with the factors of production, different sizes of countries and differences in the level of their technological development. Fears and anxieties linked to migration also strengthen cultural and national differences (see chapters written by Agnieszka Konopelko and Stefania Alina Cherata). Over the past twenty five years the post-Soviet area has developed a whole system of migration. It singled out important centres in Russia and Kazakhstan which are very attractive to human resources from countries built on the collapse of the USSR. Russia, however, plays an incomparably more important role. The Russian regulations concerning migrants are an important element in the shaping of international relations. In the area of the Commonwealth of Independent States they shape the socio-economic situation in Russia and in many other countries.

It should be noted that the direction and number of immigrants in the area of the Commonwealth of Independent States are caused not only by economic factors, but also demographic ones. On the one hand, the demographic crisis in Russia and Belarus is deepening. This manifests itself in a decline in the population, especially the portion which is working age. Therefore, there are also negative qualitative changes in human resources. On the other hand, Kyrgyzstan and Tajikistan are the countries with rapidly increasing populations, and with a young age structure. Kazakhstan occupies an intermediate position between these two groups of countries. The demographic situation in the Republic of Kazakhstan deteriorated greatly in the 90s, when the population of 17 million in 1992 decreased to 15 million by 1999. The outflow of migrants played a major role in reducing the population of Kazakhstan, which, from 1992 to 2003, amounted to 2.1 million people.[17]

Kyrgyzstan and Tajikistan are being affected by economic stagnation and a significant percentage of the population is living in poverty (see Table 2: Main macroeconomic factors, especially GDP per capita), which leads to an outflow of working age population. An intermediate position is occupied by Belarus, which seems to be the provider of labour force (mainly to the Russian Federation and the Republic of Kazakhstan), as well as being its recipient.

Individual states of the Commonwealth of Independent States have different characteristics of their labour markets. However, a certain complementarity requires appropriate adjustment. Russia and Kazakhstan have a strong need for additional labour, particularly, skilled labour. At the same time, there is a unique situation on the labour markets in Kyrgyzstan and Tajikistan. It is caused by excess of workforce across the country while at the same time there are also clear signs of a shortage of workforce in rural areas. Uncontrolled migration is a threat to all the countries of the CIS as it leads to the formation and development of informal and black labour market, it fosters corruption (e.g. in the Russian Federation) as well as organized crime (e.g. in Tajikistan).

In the liberalization of freedom of movement, the post-Soviet states have aimed at finding a solution to problems related to migrations. According to various statistics, each year up to two million citizens of the former Soviet republics arrive at the Russian Federation in search for work (with the exception of Belarus).[18] In extreme cases, namely Kyrgyzstan and Tajikistan, the money earned by migrants abroad is, according to various estimates, nearly half of the revenue of their countries. This means that the poorer countries care particularly about their freedom of access to the Russian labour market. Any changes to the Russian

Federation migration laws cause concern in many post-Soviet countries. In this context, they favour the integration with Russia. However, Russian goodwill coming from RIAs may only mean a partial solution to the social problems in many countries of the Commonwealth of Independent States. The Customs Union (a part of the Eurasian Economic Community) is an example of that.

The formation of first the Customs Union by Russia, Belarus and Kazakhstan, and then the Common Economic Space led to the signing of and hence coming into force the following agreements:

- an agreement on the legal status of workers - migrants and members of their families,
- an agreement on cooperation in the prevention of illegal migration from third countries.[19]

These sped the transition to a qualitatively different level of interstate relations, characterized by free movement of workers within the Common Economic Space. The legal status of migrant workers of the CES Member States allows citizens of Russia, Kazakhstan and Belarus to realize their right to work in each of the three countries without any restrictions that usually apply to foreign workers. Their right to work is now fully regulated by the labour law which does not classify employees on the grounds of their nationality.

The removal of borders in the Customs Union and the Common Economic Space between Russia, Kazakhstan and Belarus raised a question of the inclusion of Kyrgyzstan and Tajikistan in the CES; currently, Armenia is undergoing its accession to the Eurasian Economic Union. In line with the former Eurasian Economic Community this step had to be taken. The enlarged CES will contribute to the legalization of migration flows between the member countries, while the impact on the border transfer and custom controls at the external borders of will help create a more tangible barrier to international drug trafficking, for which Tajikistan is infamous.

The majority of work is to ensure welfare of migrants, the creation of an effective system of tax and migration control. Moscow must also face the problem of assimilation of individual groups of visitors and crime occurring in these environments. It must also protect the southern border against drug trafficking.

5. Conclusion

There are many economic and political problems in the post-Soviet region generating different fears and anxieties. In the contemporary globalized world, economic and political integration with a strong country or a group of countries seems to be essential. The Russian Federation, through regional integration, offers some predictable stability to many countries of the post-Soviet region.

It is very difficult to say whether regional economic integration can be a driving factor revitalizing economies of the post-Soviet countries and thus, if it is likely to be the remedy for the many fears and anxieties in this region.

What seems clear, is the fact that these countries are mutually complementary in many areas. However, regardless of their fears and anxieties, they need to develop different forms of cooperation, dependence associated with labour markets is a good example. Many nations of Eurasia are afraid of the restrictions regarding access to the Russian labour market. The Russians, by contrast, are afraid of a considerable influx of people from the outside. However, post-Soviet countries, in some sense, are condemned to each other.

The migration policy of the Russian Federation, approved on June 13, 2012 until 2025, was created to meet the challenges regarding the labour market between the Russian Federation and other CIS countries. It was developed by the Federal Migration Service.[20] The Russian Federation suffers from a shortage of workforce brought about with, among other things, negative population growth and outflow of skilled workforce. It also lacks workers who can carry out the most basic work unattractive for the Russians. Therefore, the document is a response to a real need of the Russian economy and its labour market. According to forecasts by experts from the Russian Academy of Sciences, within the next five years, the number of economically active population in Russia will decrease by about 1 million a year . Therefore the flow of people from the outside is essential otherwise the Russian Federation will not be able to overcome the negative trend.

Besides the economic problems in the analyzed region, fears and anxieties are rampant. They are connected with the fact that many areas of the post-Soviet region are characterized by significant ethnic and cultural diversity resulting in many tensions and borderline conflicts, separatism and even wars. Economic regional integration is not the solution to all of them. However, stable economic growth is a factor that may help. Various examples of regional integration such as the European Union, ASEAN (The Association of Southeast Asian Nations), and Mercosur (Mercado Común del Sur, Southern Common Market) demonstrate that growing standards of living, and growing HDI (Human Development Index) may help in solving political, and even ethnic problems. Regional integration theories, including neofunctional theory, show how this happens.

What seems quite clear, is that the regional economic integration processes within the post-Soviet area should be complementary to the European integration (mainly the EU), Asian integration (ASEAN, Association of South-East Asian Nations or APEC, Asia-Pacific Economic Co-operation, and others.) and generally should improve the level of integration of these countries with the world's economy. If the model of integration within the post-Soviet area takes a form of competition with the rest of the world, it will perpetuate the economic backwardness of this region and thus deepen the existing problems.

The Russian-Ukrainian conflict and the war in Ukraine have made all participants of international relations aware of yet another source of 'fears and anxieties' within the post-Soviet region. A deeply-rooted desire to dominate and to influence the eleven countries of post-Soviet area is an important aspect of the foreign policy of the Russian Federation. Lack of Russia' consent to any alternative visions of integration may end the process of integration of the post-Soviet region and the global economy. Such scenario would result in the escalation of fears and anxieties in this area.

Acknowledgement

The project has been financed from the National Science Centre funds awarded on the basis of Decision DEC-2011/03/B/HS4/05/930.

Notes

[1] Economic Commission for Latin America, *The Latin American Common Market and the Multilateral Payments System* (Santiago: United Nations Publications, 1959), 5.

[2] Ernst B. Haas, 'International Integration: The European and the Universal Process,' *International Organization* 15.3 (1961): 366-392.

[3] Bela Balassa, 'Towards a Theory of Economic Integration,' *Kyklos International Review of Social Sciences* 14.1 (1961): 1-17.

[4] Aleksandr Libman and Evgeny Vinokurov, *Holding-Together Integration: 20 Years of the Post-Soviet Integration* (London: Palgrave Macmillan, 2012).

[5] Dmitri Trenin, *The End of Eurasia: Russia on the Border Between Geopolitics and Globalization* (Washington: Carnegie Center, 2002).

[6] Makarychev Andrey and Viatcheslav Morozov, 'Multilateralism, Multipolarity, and Beyond: A Menu of Russia's Policy Strategies,' *Global Governance: A Review of Multilateralism and International Organizations* 17.3 (2011): 353-373; Stanisław Bieleń and Maciej Raś, *Polityka Zagraniczna Rosji* [*Russian Foreign Policy*] (Warszawa: Difin, 2008).

[7] Aleksandr Libman, *Studies of Regional Integration in the CIS and in Central Asia: A Literature Survey, Report 2* (Saint Petersburg: Eurasian Development Bank, 2012).

[8] Walter Mattli, *The Logic of Regional Integration: Europe and Beyond* (Cambridge: Cambridge University Press, 1999).

[9] Ismee Tames, 'Expecting War in Europe: Fears an Anxieties about War,' in *Fears and Anxieties in the 21st Century: The European Context and Beyond*, ed. Catalin Ghita and Robert Beshara (Oxford: Inter-Disciplinary Press, 2015).

[10] Katarzyna Czerewacz and Zofia Tomczonek, 'The Scope and Character of International Relations in the Central Asia,' *International Review of Business Research Papers (IRBRP) Journal* 4.2 (2008): 65-73.

[11] Agnieszka Konopelko, in this volume.

[12] Konopelko, in this volume.

[13] Maciej Raś, *Ewolucja Polityki Zagranicznej Rosji wobec Stanów Zjednoczonych i Europy Zachodniej w latach 1991-2001* [*Evolution of the Russian Federation's Foreign Policy Toward the United States and Western Europe in the Years 1991-2001*] (Warsaw: Warsaw University Press, 2005), 17.

[14] Trenin, *The End of Eurasia,* 5-7.

[15] European Commission, Directorate - General for Trade, viewed on 8 October 2014, http://ec.europa.eu/trade/policy/countries-and-regions/countries/russia/.

[16] Stefania Alina Cherata in this volume.

[17] Katarzyna Czerewacz-Filipowicz, 'Migration Policy as a Functional Platform of Economic Integration within the Eurasian Economic Community,' *Economics and Law*, Vol. XII, No. 1(2013): 62; Владимир Алексеевич Ионцев, Ирина Валентиновна Ивахнюк, Алла Витальевна Магомедова, Иван Андреевич. Алешковский, Юлия Анатольевна Прохорова, Наталия Владимировна. Шевченко, Владимир Глод, 'Единый рынок труда в ЕЭП: экономический эффект согла-шений в области трудовой миграции,' Евразийская экономическая интеграция. Научно-аналитический журнал. No 2 (2012): 8.

[18] Ibid., 10.

[19] Czerewacz-Filipowicz, 'Migration Policy,' 63-64.

[20] Concept of the State Migration Policy of the Russian Federation through to 2025, *The Kremlin* website, viewed on 5 May 2014, http://www.kremlin.ru.

Bibliography

Balassa, Bela. 'Towards a Theory of Economic Integration.' *Kyklos International Review of Social Sciences* 14.1 (1961): 1-17.

Bieleń, Stanisław and Maciej Raś. *Polityka zagraniczna Rosji* [*Russian Foreign Policy*]. Warszawa: Difin, 2008.

Concept of the State Migration Policy of the Russian Federation through to 2025, *The Kremlin* website. Viewed on 5 May 2014. http://www.kremlin.ru.

Czerewacz, Katarzyna and Zofia Tomczonek. 'The Scope and Character of International Relations in the Central Asia.' *International Review of Business Research Papers (IRBRP) Journal* 4.2 (2008): 65-73.

Czerewacz-Filipowicz, Katarzyna. 'Migration Policy as a Functional Platform of Economic Integration within the Eurasian Economic Community.' *Economics and Law* XII.1 (2013): 57-67.

Economic Commission for Latin America. *The Latin American Common Market and the Multilateral Payments System.* Santiago: United Nations Publication, 1959.

European Commission, Directorate - General for Trade. Viewed on 8 October 2014. http://ec.europa.eu/trade/policy/countries-and-regions/countries/russia/.

Haas Ernst B. 'International Integration: The European and the Universal Process.' *International Organization* 15.3 (1961): 366-392.

International Monetary Fund. World Economic Outlook Database, April 2014. Viewed on 15 July 2014.
http://www.imf.org/external/pubs/ft/weo/2014/01/weodata/index.aspx.

Ионцев, Владимир Алексеевич, Ивахнюк Ирина Валентиновна, Магомедова Алла Витальевна., Алешковский Иван Андреевич., Прохорова Юлия Анатольевна, Шевченко Наталия Владимировна, Глод Владимир, 'Единый рынок труда в ЕЭП: экономический эффект соглашений в области трудовой миграции,' ['A Single Labour Market in the CES: The Economic Effect of Labour Migration Agreements] *Евразийская экономическая интеграция. Научно-аналитический журнал.* No 2.15 (2012): 6-24.

Libman, Aleksandr. *Studies of Regional Integration in the CIS and in Central Asia: a Literature Survey, Report 2.* Saint Petersburg: Eurasian Development Bank, 2012.

Libman, Aleksandr, and Evgeny Vinokurov. *Holding-Together Integration: 20 Years of the Post-Soviet Integration.* London: Palgrave Macmillan, 2012.

Mattli, Walter. *The Logic of Regional Integration: Europe and Beyond.* Cambridge University Press 1999.

Makarychev, Andrey, and Viatcheslav Morozov. 'Multilateralism, Multipolarity, and Beyond: A Menu of Russia's Policy Strategies.' *Global Governance: A Review of Multilateralism and International Organizations* 17.3 (2011): 353-373.

Raś, Maciej. *Ewolucja Polityki Zagranicznej Rosji wobec Stanów Zjednoczonych i Europy Zachodniej w latach 1991-2001 [Evolution of the Russian Federation's Foreign Policy Toward the United States and Western Europe in the Years 1991-2001].* Warsaw: Warsaw University Press, 2005.

Trenin, Dmitri. *The End of Eurasia: Russia on the Border between Geopolitics and Globalization.* Washington: Carnegie Center, 2001.

Katarzyna Czerewacz-Filipowicz works at Bialystok University of Technology, Faculty of Management, Department of Economics and Social Sciences. Her main area of interest is regional integration agreements (RIAs), with a special consideration of the post-Soviet area (the CIS, the Eurasian Economic Union, the Customs Union).

Afraid of the Other: The Untimely Character of Patriotic Poetry

Catalin Ghita

Abstract
The premise of my chapter, read in a broadly comparative cultural context, is that the values of patriotic poetry have acquired an untimely character and that love of one's own country underlies fear of another's, which may be combined with such attitudes as racial and/or ethnic superiority, moral self-justification and economic selfishness. I intend to read this subtle fear of otherness in terms of a clash between the self and the Other (l'Autrui), who is the absolute Stranger, as posited by Emmanuel Levinas in *Totality and Infinity* (*Totalité et infini*). Although intellectual curiosity prompts one to seek to discover the Other, our fragile world is permanently menaced and even torn apart by the fact that fear of ontological displacement drives one to uphold her/his own familiar principles and beliefs and reject the values and ways of life of the Other. After defining these terms and their complex relationship, it is my intention to examine a few relevant literary contexts (mainly, inflammatory poems written in various European languages: English, French and German, on the one hand, and Serbian, Romanian, Bulgarian and Russian, on the other) that reveal and exacerbate the afore-mentioned confrontation. Because of the didactic function of literature, which is, after all, the cornerstone of general education in school and therefore a firm, if somewhat biased, depository of axiology, I hold that the traditional teaching of patriotic values under the auspices of literary studies subverts the very foundations of the cosmopolitan world that post-WW2 humanistic ideals have continuously sought to establish and defend.

Key Words: Fear, otherness, alterity, patriotism, nationalism, European poetry, danger.

*****

1. Two Elusive Concepts: Patriotism vs. Nationalism

From the very onset of one's analysis, one may note that it is notoriously hard to define the two key terms which have shaped the lives of so many people throughout the last couple of centuries. However, some useful tools may be at hand, and, in order to shape a more convincing discourse, I had better examine them one by one.

In his hugely influential study on the origin and dissemination of nationalism, titled *Imagined Communities* (first published in 1983), Benedict Anderson emphasizes from the very onset of his analysis that the widely spread concepts of 'nation', 'nationality' and 'nationalism' 'have proved notoriously difficult to define, let alone to analyse. In contrast to the immense influence that nationalism has exerted on the modern world, plausible theory about it is conspicuously meagre'.[1]

In his scholarly attempt to clarify the hazy term, Anderson starts from the working hypothesis that nationality and nationalism 'are cultural artefacts of a particular kind',[2] which emerged in the late eighteenth century. Once created, Anderson opines, the terms became 'modular', i.e. able to be transferred and applied to various social and ethnic varieties, according to the specific conditions of the respective communities.

In an anthropological vein, Anderson subsequently offers his own synthetic definition of a nation: 'an imagined political community'.[3] A nation is imagined 'because the members of even the smallest nation will never know most of their fellow-members, meet them, or even hear of them, yet in the minds of each lives the image of their communion'.[4] In contrast to Ernest Gellner's interpretation of invented nations as fabricated or false communities,[5] Anderson believes that the collective representation of a nation is an act of imagination, of creation: 'Communities are to be distinguished, not by their falsity/genuineness, but by the style in which they are imagined'.[6]

The legitimate question which arises becomes disconcertingly simple: is there a difference between nationalism and patriotism? It is still hard to come up with a clear-cut answer. In the prestigious *Stanford Encyclopedia of Philosophy*, Igor Primoratz deplores the elusive character of patriotism as a notion and emphasizes that '[d]iscussions of both patriotism and nationalism are often marred by lack of clarity due to the failure to distinguish the two. Many authors use the two terms interchangeably'.[7] Whilst acknowledging the same state of affairs, Ross Poole notes a slight difference, which 'lies in the evaluative tone of the two terms. "Patriotism" is more likely to be used in a positive sense, whilst "nationalism" to be used negatively'.[8]

On the other hand, Stephen Nathanson, in his study *Patriotism, Morality and Peace* (published in 1993), believes that four main ingredients are detectable in a typical patriotic attitude: emotional attachment with one's country, identifying one's personality with one's country, care for the integrity and progress of one's country and inclination towards self-sacrifice for the preservation of one's country.[9] Igor Primoratz also concludes that 'patriotism can be defined as love of one's country, identification with it, and special concern for its well-being and that of compatriots'.[10] Truth be said, this definition reiterates the one read in terms of a 'topic in moral philosophy'[11] and found in the reader on the theme, titled *Patriotism: Philosophical and Political Perspectives*, which Primoratz and Aleksandar Pavković edited in 2007.

However, if one insists on differentiating between nationalism and patriotism, one had better turn to George Orwell's essay, 'Notes on Nationalism' (1945). By 'patriotism', Orwell understands 'devotion to a particular place and a particular way of life, which one believes to be the best in the world but has no wish to force on other people',[12] adding that '[p]atriotism is of its nature defensive, both militarily and culturally'.[13] On the other hand, Orwell believes that nationalism 'is inseparable from the desire for power. The abiding purpose of every nationalist is to secure more power and more prestige, NOT (emphasis in the text) for himself but for the nation ...'.[14] Read in this interesting, if debatable, dialectic between defence and aggression and between retreat and attack, the two terms may be set apart to a certain degree. Considering Orwell's afore-discussed distinctions scientifically unsatisfactory, Maurizio Viroli resumes, in his 1997-study, *For Love of Country*, this dialectic from a different angle of interpretation: 'for the patriots, the primary value is the republic and the free way of life that the republic permits; for the nationalists, the primary values are the spiritual and cultural unity of the people'.[15]

Naturally, as in nearly all cases of philosophical discourse, the questions remain open.

2. Fear of Otherness: The Stakes of Alterity

By now, I think, the fact that I read patriotism in terms of a generic fear of alterity (One is constantly afraid of the Other, and, as history has hastened to offer ample proof to this, fear begets aggression) may, indeed, be the secret of Polichinelle. Suffice it to say that, in regard to alterity, the 20th-century French philosopher Emmanuel Levinas writes, in *Totality and Infinity: An Essay on Exteriority* (*Totalité et infini. Essai sur l'exteriorité*, first published in 1961), that '[t]he absolutely other is the Other. He and I do not form a number. The collectivity in which I say "you" or "we" is not a plural of the "I". I, you—these are not individuals of a common concept'.[16] He continues in like manner: '[n]either possession nor the unity of number nor the unity of concepts link me to the Stranger [l'Étranger], the stranger who disturbs the being at home with oneself [le chez soi]'.[17] I intend to interpret this subtle fear of otherness, which mixes both a complex of superiority and one of inferiority, construed at different semantic levels, in terms of a powerful clash between the self and the Other (with a capital letter, l'Autrui, to distinguish it from the other, l'autre), who is the absolute Stranger, as posited by Levinas. Although intellectual curiosity prompts one to seek to discover the Other, our fragile world is permanently menaced and even torn apart by the fact that fear of ontological displacement drives one to uphold her/his own familiar principles and beliefs and reject the values and ways of life of the Other. One's frustration in relation to the Other is enhanced, as Levinas points out, by the fact that the Other remains essentially unattached and uncontrollable: 'Stranger also means the free one. Over him I have no *power* (emphasis in the text). He escapes my grasp by an essential dimension, even if I have him at my disposal'.[18]

As I stated in the premise, the more one proclaims her/his love of one's country, the more it becomes evident that this inflamed rhetoric underlies her/his fear of another's. In other words, it is not so much identity of community which triggers patriotic feelings, but rather fear of the unfamiliar, the potential threat which menaces one's social habits. Being afraid of what one does not know or understand is, in fact, a preservation reflex, which is subsequently internalized and conveniently transformed into a powerful instrument of knowledge and axiology, which identifies, labels and categorizes items, be they ethnic, racial, social, cultural, religious, moral or economic. Most people inevitably tend to cling to old habits and lifeways, all with a view to not being subjected to the tyranny of diversity and, therefore, to the peril of potential loss of control. That is why the jealous defence of the familiar implies racial and/or ethnic superiority, moral self-justification and economic selfishness. All these epiphenomena of power translate an identity attitude which is expected to be exacerbated in direct proportion to some (and, in certain intellectual circles, even prevalent) current tendencies towards globalization and the embracing of truly cosmopolitan perspectives upon human reality. Recent events, such as the civil war in Ukraine and the expansion of the self-fashioned Islamic State throughout much of Syria and Iraq, are grim testimony to the fact that nationalistic attitudes, be they motivated imperially or religiously, are very much on today's political agenda and, unless prompt steps are taken, there is little doubt that they will continue to inflame spirits in the months and years to come. The advent and recent multiplication of extreme and gruesome acts of terror throughout Europe and elsewhere proves the Western society's failure to address the ills that its previous colonial expansion sadly and irresponsibly created.

There are two main internal contradictions which menace and subvert any legitimacy of patriotism (*y compris* nationalism), namely the contradiction of arbitrary birth and the ethical contradiction. The former refers to the hazard of geographic distribution experienced, at birth, by any individual: indeed, who can decide the country or territory in which she or he is brought into existence? If this is not the fruit of a deliberate choice, but the product of hazard, defending the values of one's native land appears absurd, especially in the light of universally accepted civil rights. Even if one were given the chance of opting for one particular country which may be in agreement with one's intimate living needs, one should rationally wish to *live* peacefully in that country, not *die* for it. The latter refers to the delicate moral position in which two soldiers of warring countries may be placed, in the sense that both may invoke patriotic reasons to justify their aggressive actions set against their opponent. Which of the two is right and, moreover, who can act as an absolute arbiter of the dispute? For, even though one is an invader and the other a defender, they both act in good conscience, according to the strict moral standards set by the respective societies into which they are born and educated. Other equally disturbing thoughts spring to mind once one has delved deeper into the matter.

3. Manipulation of Fear through Patriotic Discourse: The Case of Western Europe

Nowhere is fear of alterity more transparent than in the context of patriotic poetry. There are several reasons for this state of affairs: 1. the historical context, 2. the geopolitical factors and 3. the dialectic established between a complex of superiority and one of inferiority. More often than not, these reasons are deceptively mixed together.

Compared to their Eastern counterparts, Western-European examples of patriotic poetry appear less flamboyant and, therefore, less shocking, perhaps, because Occidental poets have learnt to hide their animosities and fears behind a thin veil of prudence, readily provided by the longer experience of democracy and the rule of law. (One notable exception would be Ernst Lissauer's rabid *Haßgesang gegen England*, promptly translated in the same year, 1914, as *Hymn of Hate against England*.) To this, one may add a certain sense of pride and fulfilment on the part of Westerners, who, at the time, had established a vast colonial empire, had witnessed the advent of science and technology and, in general, a considerably higher standard of living than anywhere else in the world. Frustrations were, therefore, less frequent.

I shall not start with William Blake's naïve prefatory versification to his epic poem *Milton* (1804-1808), which became, in conjunction with Sir Hubert Parry's music, a veritable English anthem, *Jerusalem*, but with a more daunting piece of poetry. An emblematic, perhaps even *the* emblematic, Victorian poet, Alfred, Lord Tennyson (1809-1892) published, in 1854, *The Charge of the Light Brigade*, a poem exalting militarism and heroism. Written at the height of Crimean War, the poem was even read by the combatants, and was subsequently turned into a mandatory cultural reference in Britain. The useless sacrifice of the mounted troops is vainly sung in exalted mantras of violence, which sound all the more ridiculous one and a half centuries later:

> Flash'd all their sabres bare,
> Flash'd as they turn'd in air,
> Sabring the gunners there,
> Charging an army, while
>
> All the world wonder'd:
> Plunged in the battery-smoke
> Right thro' the line they broke;
> Cossack and Russian
> Reel'd from the sabre-stroke
>
> Shatter'd and sunder'd.
> Then they rode back, but not,
> Not the six hundred.[19]

The British national anthem itself, the famous *God Save the King/Queen* (whichever the case may be), attributed to an otherwise obscure poet and song-writer, Henry Carey (1687-1743), is not devoid of aggressive, nationalistic tendencies and self-centredness. In an involuntarily humorous twist, one finds out that, if the monarch may be placed in the highly embarrassing position of not being able to defend their subjects, God Almighty should be peremptorily summoned to preserve their delicate, nay, sacred lives and crush those of their enemies. The median stanza proves that the Supreme Being is bound to swear loyalty to England:

> O Lord our God arise,
> Scatter her enemies,
> And make them fall:
> Confound their politics,
> Frustrate their knavish tricks,
> On Thee our hopes we fix:
> God save us all.[20]

Fortunately, the lyrics added around 1745 and directed against the 'rebellious Scots', bound to be vanquished by Field Marshal George Wade's powerful army, were tactfully, if unceremoniously, deleted from the official version of the anthem in the early 1800s.

A mere officer in the Republican army, but, no doubt, an ardent patriot and a very pious citizen, Claude-Joseph Rouget de Lisle (1760-1836) composed, in 1792, what would become the French national anthem and one of the most well-known and revered anthems in the whole world, *La Marseillaise. Battle Song for the Army of the Rhine* (*Chant de guerre pour l'armée du Rhin*),[21] as its original title sounded, is a paean to nationalistic supremacy, to ethnic cleansing, as well as an overt instigation to war. Especially the metaphor of 'impure blood' in the refrain is chilling:

> In the countryside, do you hear
> The roaring of these fierce soldiers?
> They come right to our arms
> To slit the throats of our sons, our friends!
>
> *Refrain*
> *Grab your weapons, citizens!*
> *Form your batallions!*
> *Let us march! Let us march!*
> *May impure blood*
> *Water our fields!*[22]

For all accounts and purposes, Ernst Moritz Arndt (1769-1860) was Rouget de Lisle's German counterpart (not a soldier, though, but an academic, as befits a German): an equally fierce patriot, who went into exile because of his staunch anti-Napoleonic stance. In 1813, he penned *What Is the German Fatherland? (Was ist des Deutschen Vaterland?)*, which quickly established itself as an a *sui generis* German anthem, recited by common folk in beer gardens. Just like its French opposite, it abounds in examples of ethnic superiority and even anticipates the Nazi set phrases, full of German oaths, of Aryan sparkling eyes and of anti-Gallic sentiment:

> There is the German's fatherland,
> Where oaths attest the grasped hand,—
> Where truth beams from the sparkling eyes,
> And in the heart love warmly lies;—
> That is the land,—
> There, brother, is thy fatherland!
>
> That is the German's fatherland,
> Where wrath pursues the foreign band,—
> Where every Frank is held a foe,
> And Germans all as brothers glow;—
> That is the Land,—
> All Germany's thy fatherland![23]

The most rabid lyrics in the history of Western patriotic poetry properly belong to the less than successful poet and dramatist Ernst Lissauer (1882-1937), who, in 1914, published *Hymn of Hate against England (Haßgesang gegen England)*. Ironically enough, Lissauer, a friend of the illustrious Stefan Zweig's, was born into a Jewish family and, though promptly decorated by the pompous Kaiser Wilhem II for his nationalistic rhymed feat, he ended up regretting his having published it. The lyrics need not be commented upon – their message is clear enough:

> French and Russian, they matter not,
> A blow for a blow, a shot for a shot,
> We fight the battle with bronze and steel,
> And the time that is coming Peace will seal.
> You we will hate with a lasting hate,
> We will never forego our hate,
> Hate by water and hate by land,
> Hate of the head and hate of the hand,
> Hate of the hammer and hate of the crown,

Hate of seventy millions choking down.
We love as one, we hate as one,
We have one foe and one alone--
ENGLAND! [24]

Further examples may be selected almost at random from various other Western authors, and they all add up to the same conclusion, which was astutely formulated by the famous French intellectual Julien Benda. In his 1927-hit, *The Treason of the Intellectuals* (*La Trahison des Clercs*), he noticed that '[p]atriotism is, today, the affirmation of one form of soul against other forms of soul'.[25] He properly added that 'this form of patriotism is new in history. It is obviously related to the adoption of this passion by the masses and seems to have been inaugurated by Germany in 1813'.[26] This form of 'democratic patriotism', Benda demonstrated, had been absent in European history, from Ancient Rome to Louis XIV's France. Herein, one may say, lie the poisoned seeds of the two World Wars which rocked our recent history. And, ironically enough, though the *casus belli* in the case of both WWI and WWII may lie in Eastern Europe (the problems of Serbia and of Poland, respectively), the main actors that precipitated the human tragedy were Westerners.

4. Manipulation of Fear through Patriotic Discourse: The Case of Eastern Europe

There is a sensitive difference between patriotic poetic discourse in Western and Eastern Europe (particularly in the Balkans, a term which should not be perceived as a derogatory toponym). A case in point is Robert D. Kaplan's astute assertion, according to which, '[i]n the Balkans, history is not viewed as tracing a chronological progression, as in the West. Instead, history jumps around and moves in circles; and where history is perceived in such a way, myths take root'.[27] A convoluted mythology, which serves as an imaginary referential basis for all contending parties, replaces cold fact. And poetry, with its flamboyant paraphernalia, made up of catchy tropes, is a natural breeder of emotions, which can only exacerbate public perception of a certain social or political occurrence. And pistols flashed in verse are not late in flashing in real life. And all this for the sake of patriotism...

The reader interested in the more practical aspects of socio-political realities in Eastern Europe should refer to Agnieszka Konopelko's chapter, 'The Case of Transnistria in the Context of the Russian Eurasian Union Project'[28].

In the following lines, just as I did in the case of Western literary examples, I shall focus on a few famous poems, written by equally famous (in their own right, that is) Eastern European authors, all of them focusing on the subtle, if devious, relationship between fear and hatred in relation to foreigners (those absolute Others, in Levinas's terminology). Whilst generally acceptable in literary theory, the thesis of the autonomy of the aesthetic does not function very well in the case of patriotic poetry, because this particular type of verse is not at all innocent from an ideological point of view, being created with a view to stirring intense feelings in the reader's psyche. Patriotism, at times subtly, at times grossly, manipulates people's fear of alterity, whilst instilling in the audience a sentiment of insecurity as regards what one may call the outer barbarians that come to reify *extra muros* danger. Thus, whatever was dangerous in the West becomes all the more so in the East. My thesis will become clearer in the subsequent brief process of literary exegesis.

Prevalent Balkan emotions of fear-induced hatred against the 'pagan' or the 'unbeliever', construed as a despicable Muslim, are vivid in the poetry of the 'national' Serb poet, prince-bishop Petar II Petrović-Njegoš (1813-1851). His acknowledged masterpiece, *The Mountain Wreath* (*Gorski vijenac*), opens with the Bishop Danilo's derisory portrait of Ottomans: 'Lo the devil with seven scarlet cloaks,/with two swords and with two crowns on his head,/the great-grandchild of the Turk, with Koran!'.[29] The Montenegrins who converted to Islam are subsequently cursed in this manner: 'May God strike you, loathsome degenerates,/why do we need the Turk's faith among us?'.[30] As if fear and hatred of foreigners were not enough, misogynistic attitudes promptly surface. To Tomas Martinović's naïve query, 'but who would dare even to imagine/a Serbian woman marrying a Turk?'[31], Knez Rogan dutifully replies: 'A woman cares not about a man's faith./A hundred times she would change religion/to accomplish what her heart desires'.[32] Finally, Voivode Batrić reveals the grim fate of all those 'pagans' who have refused conversion to Christianity: 'We put under our sharp sabres all those/who did not want to be baptized by us'.[33] Further details are equally relevant: 'We set on fire all the Turkish houses,/that there might be not a single trace left/of our faithless domestic enemy'.[34]

The Romanian national anthem, called *Awaken Thee, Romanian* (*Deasteapta-te, romane*) is replete with vengeful and violent images, some of which reify a century-old paranoid feeling, according to which the whole world conspires against the union of the three Romanian provinces, sadly divided until the merging of the first two, Wallachia and Moldavia, in 1859, and later joined by Transylvania, in 1918:

> Romanians from the four corners, now or never
> Unite in thought, unite in feeling
> Proclaim to the wide world that the Danube is stolen
> Through intrigue and coercion, sly machinations.[35]

The fact that the author of these lyrics, the poet Andrei Muresanu (1816-1863), penned this poem in 1848, the pan-European revolutionary year, accounts for the hagiographic image, in the final stanza, of the priests armed with crosses. (In that *annus mirabilis*, it seemed everyone was to be forgiven, except the Others, the foreigners.) Somehow, most people have overlooked the simple fact that a Christian *army* is a contradiction in terms: 'Priests, lead with your crucifixes, for our army is Christian'.[36]

The late romantic Mihai Eminescu (1850-1889), widely considered to be the 'national' Romanian poet (and turned into a vivid cultural icon because of his early and mysterious demise), wrote a chauvinist poem called *Doina*, an untranslatable noun denoting a tune style, specific to Romanian folk music. *Doina* is an epitome of xenophobic rhymed verse, expressing the deeply-embedded feeling of mistrust nurtured by a whole community, then unexposed to minimally democratic beliefs, and directed against the illusory menace of all foreigners. The first quatrain is eloquent enough:

> From Tisa to the Nistru's tide
> All Romania's people cried
> That they could no longer stir
> For the rabbled foreigner.[37]

Subsequent verses identify the peril to the intergrity and purity of one's nation – this comes to be reified by Russians, for instance:

> From Hotin down to the sea
> Rides the Muscal cavalry;
> From the sea back to Hotin
> Nothing but their host is seen.[38]

The poem ends with a diatribe, a destructive curse, unparalleled and indomitable in its general tone:

> Who has sent them [the foreigners] to these parts,
> May the dogs eat out their hearts;
> May the night their homes efface,
> And with them this shameless race.[39]

Ivan Vazov (1850-1921), again, the 'national' author of Bulgarian literature, an accomplished poet, novelist and playwright, penned a series of exalted poems, published under the aegis of a nationalist saga, in its turn, dedicated to the memory of almost-forgotten heroes of the past. The collection's title is *Epic of the Forgotten* (*Epopeya na zabravenite*) and one may select numerous examples of chauvinist attitudes and xenophobic rhetoric. A case in point is *Paissy*, a poem devoted to the prophetic personality of monk Paissy Hilendarski, an 18th-century historian. Thanks to him, it appears, young Bulgarians must bear in mind that it is their duty to hate the Greeks:

> May all our brothers read here and remember
> That Greeks are perfidious people and clever,
> That we have repulsed them – and more than once –
> That's why they can't stomach the likes of us.[40]

It is striking how much the general tone of the imprecations resemble that employed by Eminescu in his *Doina*:

> Woe to you, fools, who like sheep are erring,
> The poisonous potion of Greeks preferring,
> Who fell of your very own brothers ashamed
> And Hellene corruption greedily acclaim.[41]

Just like Eminescu poetically summons Stephen the Great, a famous 15th-century Moldavian hospodar and a champion of Christian war against the Ottomans, to blow his battle trumpet and gather all his subjects around his faithful sword, Vazov's Paissy demands that his fellow Bulgarians read his history book and discover with awe the power and magnificence of the old Bulgar rulers, in an epitome of patriotic hyperbole, which, needless to say, matches reality just as much as Eminescu's discourse:

> Read and discover upon these pages
> The deeds of your forebears in long-gone ages:
> How bravely with many a kingdom they fought,
> And powerful kings to them tribute brought.[42]

But probably the most shocking example of patriotism which incites to racial murder, again spurred by ethnic fear, is found in Russian literature. The aristocrat turned-revolutionary poet Konstantin Mihailovich Simonov (1915-1979) published, at the height of the German invasion of the Soviet Union in the second world war, a devastating poem, titled *Kill Him* (*Ubey yego*). To say that these lyrics incite to hatred and revenge assassination is an understatement. Whilst the mood in which the verse was composed by the highly decorated war poet is completely understandable – it is too easy to forget, in today's pacific European Union, the widespread atrocities perpetrated by the Wehrmacht and particularly the Waffen SS and the Einsatzgruppen in the republics of the Soviet Union –, the general message of the poem, which would translate as 'kill each and every German available', is blood-curdling. In the first part of the poem, one's house,

one's garden, then one's family are quickly brought into the powerful equation of
hate and wrath:

> If you don't want to give away
> To a German with his black gun
> Your house, your mother, your wife
> No: No one will save your land
> If you don't save it from the worst.
> No: No one will kill this foe,
> If you don't kill him first.[43]

In the second part of the poem, a sort of killing competition arises among peer
soldiers, eager to demonstrate that they can emulate Hitler's armies insofar as
criminal zeal is concerned:

> If your brother killed a German,
> If your neighbor killed one too,
> It's your brother's and neighbor's vengeance,
> And it's no revenge for you.
> You can't sit behind another
> Letting him fire your shot.
> If your brother kills a German,
> He's a soldier; you are not.
>
> So kill that German so he
> Will lie on the ground's backbone,
> So the funeral wailing will be
> In his house, not in your own.
> He wanted it so it's his guilt
> Let his house burn up, and his life.
> Let his woman become a widow;
> Don't let it be your wife.
> Don't let your mother tire from tears;
> Let the one who bore him bear the pain.
> Don't let it be yours, but his
> Family who will wait in vain.[44]

The concluding quatrain re-emphasizes, if need be, the extremely aggressive
message of the poem. One is forced to kill the Other for fear that the Other might
kill him first:

So kill at least one of them
And as soon as you can. Still
Each one you chance to see!
Kill him! Kill him! Kill![45]

All the lyrics reproduced so far emphasize my premise, that love of one's country is a mask for fear of another, expressed in terms of suspicion, disdain or hatred. In all instances, it is immediately obvious that nationalist authors posit intrinsic ethnic and moral superiority on the part of their fellow countrymen. All the poems from which I have selected the afore-mentioned quotes (especially those composed in Eastern Europe before and even during the advent of communism, which were quickly converted into instruments of nationalistic propaganda) have been widely quoted in school and, in certain cases, even learnt by heart by enthusiastic pupils, who have had few tools to defend their innocence against this kind of ethnic and moral manipulation. The result is that, instead of ruling out war completely as a means of settling territorial disputes, new generations tend to repeat the mistakes done by their parents and grandparents in the past and start up new wars with old slogans.

5. A Cosmopolitan World or a Myriad of Ever-Warring Nations?

It has become, by now, abundantly clear that, if it is to have a future at all, our world should embrace cosmopolitan values and, consequently, subordinate the particular to the general, or the love of one's country to the love of humanity as a whole. Aleksandar Pavković is, I believe, essentially right when he asserts that '[k]illing for one's country may indeed be an expression of love and frustration at the removal of the object of patriotic love. But it is also a political act, aiming at a political outcome'.[46] And that outcome, one is bound to add, is frustratingly narrow and limited.

Humanity has always defined itself through division and conquest (the old and practical Roman adage is not, after all, a catchy journalistic formula, but a sad fact of life). The feeble excuses made for the afore-mentioned actions used to be religious, to which one added, after the immense uproar caused by the dissemination of nationalistic ideas (which were, after all, the brain child of the romantic age), ethnic (therefore, patriotic), issues. If violence is a defining trait of our species, then it is not in our best interest to preserve and, in some instances, even to boost the narrow moral standards of defending one's 'sacred flag'. How difficult is it to observe that a propensity for external aggression, which has helped humanity establish itself as the dominant species on this planet, is always there, constantly looking for expressive outlets, such as belief in gods or in national states? Instead of seeking an elusive solution for ending all wars (this refrain was repeated more than one hundred years ago, when Europe prepared itself for an absurd act of collective suicide) and establishing Edenic, universal peace without dismantling the complex statal apparatus which has allowed most individuals to foster deceptively parochial ideas and interests, humanity had better look elsewhere for pacific panacea. Herein lies yet another trap which freedom of thought and freedom of expression have inadvertently, albeit inevitable, created: the world can indeed function as a whole and adopt democratic values only when the individuals comprised in it have willingly accepted this rule of thumb. The harsh reality is that the world we live in today functions as an intellectual machine whose cogs are blocked at different stages of civilization: some people embrace pre-modern, other people – postmodern ideas. Persuading the former to embrace the latter's frame of mind would seem the logical next step towards concord: yet, in this particular case, how can we defend this group's personal freedom of choice? Libertarian discourse remains trapped within the intellectual boundaries of its own highly refined contradictions.

However, theory is one thing and practice is another. All these arguments bring me to the very core of the matter, which I insert here in lieu of a proper set of conclusive remarks, fashioned according to strict academic standards and expectations. In the absence of a generous set of world-encompassing values, regional strife and bellicose tendencies among nations will grow in intensity as weapons become more refined and, therefore, more destructive. And once weapons of mass destruction have become widely available, not only to irresponsible agents of national power, but equally to rogue regional factions, inclined to use them upon what they perceive to be enemy groups and communities, the lack of a global control and sanction of these, as well as an orientation towards parochial interests go against the common good of us all. Which, in this case, constitutes the very survival of our species.

The age of national states is all but gone, and we can glimpse the advent of another structural identity of human communities. Meanwhile, how long will it take us all to understand that one is not born English, Algerian, Brazilian or Chinese, but simply a human being?

Notes

[1] Benedict Anderson, *Imagined Communities: Reflections on the Origin and Spread of Nationalism* (London: Verso, 2006), 3.
[2] Ibid., 4.
[3] Ibid., 6.
[4] Ibid., 6.
[5] For additional details, see Ernest Gellner, *Thought and Change* (London: Weidenfeld and Nicolson, 1964), 169.
[6] Anderson, *Imagined Communities*, 6.

[7] Igor Primoratz, 'Patriotism', in *The Stanford Encyclopedia of Philosophy* (Fall 2013 Edition), ed. Edward N. Zalta, viewed on 8 October 2014, http://plato.stanford.edu/archives/fall2013/entries/patriotism/.

[8] Ross Poole, 'Patriotism and Nationalism', in *Patriotism: Philosophical and Political Perspectives*, ed. Igor Primoratz and Aleksandar Pavković (Aldershot, Hampshire and Burlington, VT: Ashgate, 2007), 129.

[9] For additional details, see Stephen Nathanson, *Patriotism, Morality, and Peace* (Lanham: Rowman & Littlefield, 1993), 34-35.

[10] Primoratz, 'Patriotism'.

[11] Igor Primoratz, 'Patriotism and Morality: Mapping the Terrain', in *Patriotism: Philosophical and Political Perspectives*, ed. Igor Primoratz and Aleksandar Pavković (Aldershot, Hampshire and Burlington, VT: Ashgate, 2007), 34.

[12] George Orwell, 'Notes on Nationalism,' *Fifty Essays*, A Project Gutenberg of Australia eBook, viewed on 8 October 2014, http://gutenberg.net.au/ebooks03/0300011h.html#part30.

[13] Ibid.

[14] Ibid.

[15] Maurizio Viroli, *For Love of Country: An Essay on Patriotism and Nationalism* (Oxford: Clarendon Press, 1997), 2.

[16] Emmanuel Levinas, *Totality and Infinity: An Essay on Exteriority*, trans. Alphonso Lingis (Pittsburgh, PA: Duquesne University Press, 2011), 39.

[17] Ibid.

[18] Ibid., 40.

[19] *Poems of Patriotism*, edited by G.K.A. Bell (London: Routledge and New York: Button, 1907), 186.

[20] *God Save the Queen*, viewed on 23 January 2015, http://www.britannica.com/EBchecked/topic/236663/God-Save-the-Queen.

[21] All versions of poems written in foreign languages will be offered in their English translation.

[22] Claude-Joseph Rouget de Lisle, *La Marseillaise*, trans. Laura K. Lawless, viewed on 22 January 2015, http://french.about.com/library/weekly/aa071400ma.htm.

[23] Ernst Moritz Arndt, *The German Fatherland*, unknown translator, viewed on 22 January 2015, http://germanhistorydocs.ghi-dc.org/docpage.cfm?docpage_id=153.

[24] Ernst Lissauer, *Hymn of Hate against England*, trans. Barbara Henderson, viewed on 22 January 2015, http://www.hschamberlain.net/kriegsaufsaetze/hassgesang.html.

[25] Julien Benda, *La Trahison des Clercs*, 106. Version numérique de Pierre Palpant, viewed on 23 January 2015

http://classiques.uqac.ca/classiques/benda_julien/trahison_des_clercs/benda_trahis
on_clercs.pdf.
Translation is mine.
[26] Ibid., 107.
[27] Robert D. Kaplan, *Balkan Ghosts: A Journey through History* (New York: Picador, St. Martin's Press, 2005), 58.
[28] Agnieszka Konopelko, 'The Case of Transnistria in the Context of the Russian Eurasian Union Project'. In this volume.
[29] Petar II Petrović-Njegoš, The Mountain Wreath, trans. Vasa D. Mihailović, viewed on 8 October 2014,
http://www.rastko.org.rs/knjizevnost/umetnicka/njegos/mountain_wreath.html.
[30] Ibid.
[31] Ibid.
[32] Ibid.
[33] Ibid.
[34] Ibid.
[35] Andrei Muresanu, *Awaken Thee Romanian*, unknown translator, viewed on 23 January 2015,
http://en.wikipedia.org/wiki/De%C8%99teapt%C4%83-te,_rom%C3%A2ne!.
[36] Ibid.
[37] Mihai Eminescu, *Doina*, trans. Corneliu M. Popescu, viewed on 8 October 2014,
http://www.gabrielditu.com/eminescu/doina.asp.
[38] Ibid.
[39] Ibid.
[40] Ivan Vazov, *Paissy*, trans. Peter Tempest, viewed on 8 October 2014,
http://www.slovo.bg/showwork.php3?AuID=283&WorkID=10653&Level=2.
[41] Ibid.
[42] Ibid.
[43] Konstantin Mihailovich Simonov, *Kill Him*, trans. Vladimir Markov and Merrill Sparks, viewed on 8 October 2014
http://www.liveleak.com/view?i=6a0_1366841683.
[44] Ibid.
[45] Ibid.
[46] Pavković, 'Killing for One's Country', 234.

Bibliography

Anderson, Benedict. *Imagined Communities: Reflections on the Origin and Spread of Nationalism*. London: Verso, 2006.

Arndt, Ernst Moritz. *The German Fatherland*. Unknown translator. Viewed on 22 January 2015.
http://germanhistorydocs.ghi-dc.org/docpage.cfm?docpage_id=153.

Bell, G. K. A., ed. *Poems of Patriotism*. London: Routledge and New York: Button, 1907.

Benda, Julien. *La Trahison des Clercs*. Version numérique de Pierre Palpant. Viewed on 23 January 2015.
http://classiques.uqac.ca/classiques/benda_julien/trahison_des_clercs/benda_trahis on_clercs.pdf.

Eminescu, Mihai. *Doina*. Translated by Corneliu M. Popescu. Viewed on 8 October 2014.
http://www.gabrielditu.com/eminescu/doina.asp.

God Save the Queen. Viewed on 23 January 2015.
http://www.britannica.com/EBchecked/topic/236663/God-Save-the-Queen.

Kaplan, Robert D. *Balkan Ghosts: A Journey through History*. New York: Picador, St. Martin's Press, 2005.

Levinas, Emmanuel. *Totality and Infinity: An Essay on Exteriority*. Translated by Alphonso Lingis. Pittsburgh, PA: Duquesne University Press, 2011.

Lissauer, Ernst. *Hymn of Hate against Engla*nd. Translated by Barbara Henderson. Viewed on 22 January 2015.
http://www.hschamberlain.net/kriegsaufsaetze/hassgesang.html.

Muresanu, Andrei. *Awaken Thee Romanian*. Unknown translator. Viewed on 23 January 2015,
http://en.wikipedia.org/wiki/De%C8%99teapt%C4%83-te,_rom%C3%A2ne!.

Natanson, Stephen. *Patriotism, Morality, and Peace*. Lanham: Rowman & Littlefield, 1993.

Orwell, George. 'Notes on Nationalism'. In George Orwell. *Fifty Essays*. A Project Gutenberg of Australia. Viewed on 8 October 2014.
http://gutenberg.net.au/ebooks03/0300011h.html#part30.

Pavković, Aleksandar. 'Killing for One's Country'. In *Patriotism: Philosophical and Political Perspectives*, edited by Igor Primoratz and Aleksandar Pavković, 219-234. Aldershot, Hampshire and Burlington, VT: Ashgate, 2007.

Petrović-Njegoš, Petar II. The Mountain Wreath. Translated by Vasa D. Mihailović. Viewed on 8 October 2014.
http://www.rastko.org.rs/knjizevnost/umetnicka/njegos/mountain_wreath.html.

Poole, Ross. 'Patriotism and Nationalism.' In *Patriotism: Philosophical and Political Perspectives*, edited by Igor Primoratz and Aleksandar Pavković, 129-145. Aldershot, Hampshire and Burlington, VT: Ashgate, 2007.

Primoratz, Igor and Aleksandar Pavković, eds. *Patriotism: Philosophical and Political Perspectives*. Aldershot, Hampshire and Burlington, VT: Ashgate, 2007.

Primoratz, Igor. 'Patriotism'. *The Stanford Encyclopedia of Philosophy* (Fall 2013 Edition), edited by Edward N. Zalta. Viewed on 8 October 2014.
http://plato.stanford.edu/archives/fall2013/entries/patriotism/.

———. 'Patriotism and Morality: Mapping the Terrain'. In *Patriotism: Philosophical and Political Perspectives*, edited by Igor Primoratz and Aleksandar Pavković, 17-35. Aldershot, Hampshire and Burlington, VT: Ashgate, 2007.

Rouget de Lisle, Claude-Joseph. *La Marseillaise*. Translated by Laura K. Lawless. Viewed on 22 January 2015,
http://french.about.com/library/weekly/aa071400ma.htm.

Simonov, Konstantin Mihailovich. *Kill Him*. Translated by Vladimir Markov and Merrill Sparks. Viewed on 8 October 2014.
http://www.liveleak.com/view?i=6a0_1366841683.

Vazov, Ivan. *Paissy*. Translated by Peter Tempest. Viewed on 8 October 2014.
http://www.slovo.bg/showwork.php3?AuID=283&WorkID=10653&Level=2.

Viroli, Maurizio. *For Love of Country: An Essay on Patriotism and Nationalism*. Oxford: Clarendon Press, 1997.

Catalin Ghita, PhD, Dr Habil, was a Japanese Government Scholar at Tohoku University and is now Professor of Comparative Literature and Cultural Studies at the University of Craiova, Romania. His research interests are: fear in literature, visionary poetry, romanticism and cultural exchanges between Europe and Asia.

Part II

Fear of Strangers in Our House

Genetics, Fear and Home: Gender-Conditioned Construction of Meaning

Clara Palleja-López

Abstract

Genetic research has demonstrated that some fears are inherited both in non-human and human animals. Further studies have also proven that fears can also be gender-specific, triggering different responses to particular stimuli depending on the sex of the individual. These discoveries open up new ways of interpreting icons of fear in both literature and film. Of these the house and the idea of *home*, which can operate as symbols of women's restricted role in society, inevitably loom largest for many female writers and readers. This chapter introduces some basic notions of the latest genetic research into fear and explores whether the fear responses of readers and audiences can be conditioned by their gender. By reviewing a series of haunted house narratives authored by male and female authors, it is shown that understandings of the haunted house differ significantly between men and women.

Key Words: Gender-specific responses, haunted house, inherited fears, interpretation, spatial restriction.

*****

A major change in the conventions of the haunted house story took place in the last decades of the twentieth century: the appearance of the evil house. Before this moment, stories about hauntings normally revolved around ghosts or demons rather than focusing on buildings themselves. Ghosts were trapped on the premises as punishment for their past crimes or as captive spirits victimised by third parties. Alternatively, hauntings could be connected to Satan, demons and hell. This chapter argues that the emergence of the evil house can be in part explained by cumulative and generational gender-specific fear resulting from women's historical dependence and emotional attachment to the ideas of home and homemaking.

1. Genetics and Fear

Recent discoveries in genetic research suggest that memories related to fear and the adequate response to them might be transmitted from generation to generation. In the case of animals, this is not new, but the preferred term has been *instinct*, and more specifically *survival instinct*. Entire patterns of behaviour in animals have been explained as a blurred combination of learning from other members of the group and the particular species' instinct. The genetic transmission of instincts in animals is now widely accepted, but in the case of humans, animal instinct has traditionally been understood as accounting for a very limited amount of human conduct. Individual progress is mostly seen as the result of *intelligent learning*. As a consequence, the biological transmission of knowledge in humans has been, to a great extent, overlooked.

The reality is that humans do display behaviour that can only be caused by non-associative fears building up over generations. An illustration of this can be seen in neonates' startled response to loud noise, or the blinking of their eyes when objects suddenly approach.[1] These basic responses have traditionally been regarded as intuition, but are in fact behaviours derived from traces of genetic memory. More complex non-associative fears include: fear of animals, heights or separation, and with these fears similar internal processes are involved.[2] According to recent studies, the reason why humans are born with encoded fears is because these are passed on by our ancestors in the stathmin gene, which controls both learned and innate fear.[3]

Indeed, some fears 'may remain dormant if individuals have no traumatic experience of the relevant situation, yet manifest quickly and persistently after subjects have undergone minimal vicarious or direct trauma.'[4] Once activated, these inherited fears provoke an immediate adequate response to what, for our ancestors, was a threat. Experiments carried out with primates demonstrate that their innate fear of snakes could be triggered by a minimum of vicarious input. When non-fearful lab-reared primates were presented with a monkey displaying fear of both live and toy snakes, they were instantly conditioned with a persistent and strong fear. This fear response was learned even when the fearful model monkey was shown on videotape.[5] However, when the snakes were replaced by rabbits in a manipulated video recording, the lab-reared monkeys ignored the rabbit input and showed no fear of the rabbits, demonstrating that the animals were responding through inherited knowledge about the shape of snakes and the consequences of their bite. The authors of the study conclude that different species genetically carried and developed memories of fear:

> [There was a] blueprint for the fear module built around the deadly threat that ancestors of snakes provided to our direct ancestors, the early mammals. During further mammalian evolution, this blueprint was modified, elaborated and specialized for the ecological niches occupied by the different species.[6]

When one considers inherited fear in the case of humans, it appears that not only do humans carry this knowledge in their genes, but also that gender-specific information might be inherited. To claim that women might be preconditioned by nature to be more fearful than men may *a priori* be seen daring and politically incorrect. However, current research 'supports the hypothesis that, in the animal kingdom, females may be more sensitive to a series of potential threats than males. In other words, women may be more predisposed than men to learn the appropriate emotion for nonhuman animals that were recurrent threats over evolutionary time.'[7] In a recent study of infant fear of spiders and snakes, it was observed that girls recognised threats that for boys were not evident. The researcher projected images of spiders, snakes, flowers and mushrooms, all accompanied by either a smiling or frowning human face. Different combinations were tried on both the male and female 5 to 11-month-old infants, with resulting data showing that females seemed to have knowledge about the poisonous creatures that the males lacked: 'girls, but not boys ... looked significantly longer when a novel snake or spider was paired with a different facial emotion.'[8] When the same was done with harmless images of flowers and mushrooms aiming for identical processes of conditioning, there was no difference in the response between boys and girls.

This gender difference, according to the study, is the result of the different roles played by males and females throughout their evolution. Women were more exposed to spiders and snakes during foraging or gathering food, and their bites were potentially more dangerous to women and their children, being inferior in body size to males and therefore more vulnerable to venom. The results of this study suggest that infants possess a perceptual template that 'prepares infants, particularly female infants, to attend to fear-relevant stimuli and learn the appropriate negative emotional response for them'.[9] The fact that there is a higher incidence of female phobia of spiders and snakes, and not of modern phobias such as flying or hypodermic needles would be consistent with this theory of generational coding.[10]

Among the fears which females show greater predisposition for, are those related to spatial restriction. Situational phobias, such as claustrophobia and fear of darkness, are far more common in women than in men.[11] The fact that all ages of women scored similar high results regardless of their background and circumstances suggests that the triggering point for their fear had to be traced beyond their direct experience. In fact, according to recent scientific research, the relationship between closed spaces, animals and fear is so deeply ingrained that spatial alterations apparently affect unrelated areas of conduct such as parental instincts and procreation. A recent study has revealed that mutant female mice with an inactive stathmine gene lose not only their awareness of physical space but also their parental instinct. According to the research, this gene is in charge of promoting what has been popularly called 'helicopter mom' (protective vigilance) behaviour in mice. Female animals with an inactive gene would prove to be ineffective at caring for newborn pups, and also by not interacting cautiously with unknown peers.[12]

2. Fear and Home

Taking all of the above into consideration, it seems logical to ponder whether the male and female responses to spatial fears might be different on the basis of inherited knowledge of fears. The briefest survey of Western history is all that is required to demonstrate that the female relationship with the home has been both complex and traumatic. The boundaries of the house delineated the only physical space wherein women enjoyed a certain degree of authority. The family home was also where women devoted themselves to raising and taking care of their loved ones, which endowed the building with intense emotional implications. However, the home also involved a certain degree of captivity, being almost always subject to the constraints of male power. If the house has repeatedly down the ages been presented as this contradictory crux of fulfilment, love and anxiety, this might explain its emergence as a preeminent object of women's fear in the last decades of the twentieth century, when women become a productive part of both the publishing and film industries.

To understand the psychological struggle undergone by women writers of horror it might be helpful to appeal to analogy by looking at patriotism and the concepts of *home* and *homeland* together. Both terms are defined by their relation to an individual or a group of humans. Without these relationships based on human emotions, the two notions fade into the non-affective terms *house* and *country* (or *region*). An individual or group feels they belong within a physical surrounding which contains and protects. As a result, emotional associations based on gratitude and security are established with this unresponsive physical delimitation. One feels safe in believing that threats are to be expected from beyond protective borders, where fear is placed outside the home. In the case of homeland, we find that 'love of one's own country underlies fear of another's,' understanding this 'fear of otherness in terms of a clash between the self and the Other.'[13] However, when this balance is broken, the psychological wound of betrayal and loss is a painful one to endure. The traumatic loss of one's homeland, easily traceable in people in exile, allows little room for conciliation, the home country being irreplaceable. In a parallel way, a threat from within the protective borders of the home would present a disturbing incongruity, which ultimately would evolve into the trope of the evil home.

The horror genre provides a suitable corpus in which these gender-conditioned fears can be easily traced. Indeed, when looking at houses in horror fiction, male and female writers show key differences in the treatment of the house. Specifically, women writers appear to make use of an exclusive type of horror based on claustrophobia and psychological dependence on buildings, whereas male authors consistently rely on graphic violence, demonology or sexual perversion as the genesis for their hauntings. These differences in approach correspond nicely with the higher rate of claustrophobia and fear of darkness in women.

If recent research is correct in postulating that women experience evolutionary fears specific to their gender, we could argue that women have something akin to a negative genetic blueprint concerning the idea of houses, resulting from millennia of domestic entrapment. An implication of this theory would be that a horror text could well work on the reader's biochemistry – his or her inherited anxieties which, although obscure to the individual as no direct experience explains them, would nevertheless be present on the subconscious level.

3. The Haunted House

The house as an antagonist could not appear in Western literature until the women's position in society began to change dramatically after the Second World War. Until this turning point, it seems fair to say that there had been relatively effective spatial control of women by the patriarchal system. As this control decreased, the presence of the house in horror is intensified in women's writing, culminating in the emergence of the 'evil house' in the 1950s. Following the logic derived from the scientific experiments with primates, mice and human infants outlined above, fear would only be activated after associative patterns were established, which implies that to a certain extent the full development of the phobia could be controlled and prevented by society.

Fiction written by women before 1900 already reveals an intuition about the psychological processes surrounding the home and homemaking. These played a crucial role in the emergence of the evil haunted house as an autonomous antagonist that ultimately facilitates the disappearance of ghosts. A commonly discussed story when discussing haunted houses and women is Charlotte Perkins Gilman's *The Yellow Wallpaper* (1892), in which the figures of the ghost and the house merge into one. Lesser precursors of the evil house are Elia W. Peattie and Edith Wharton, who present the house as an active and independent force that causes destructive transformations in its occupants.

However, intelligent sentience per se was not fully developed until the publication of *The Haunting of Hill House* (1959) by Shirley Jackson. The socio-cultural context of Jackson's novel was the forcing back of American women into suburban homemaking after they had kept the country running during the Second World War. The evil house arrives at the point when women's awareness of the house's destructive potential meets the impossibility of escaping it. Hill House is the first house to be 'born evil' for no apparent reason. The house was born from the imagination of an educated woman living in suburbia who was always torn between her domestic obligations and her need for her own privacy and space.

The Haunting of Hill House opens with a powerfully descriptive paragraph which identifies the eponymous house as 'not sane.' There are four main characters. Dr John Montague, who is searching for scientific evidence of the supernatural, invites people with past experience with paranormal events to stay overnight. Of twelve people invited, only two reply: Eleanor Vance, a shy young woman who resents having grown up taking care of her invalid mother, and Theodora, a larger-than-life bohemian artist. The fourth member of the party is Luke Sanderson, the young heir to Hill House, who plays host to the others and is to supervise the experiment. Theodora has been selected because of her clairvoyant talent, something in which she is not particularly interested. Eleanor is invited for having unintentionally caused a rain of stones a few days after her father's death.

Eleanor, now homeless after her mother's loss, has been living with her married sister's family for three months when she receives the invitation. Eleanor feels resentment towards her mother and her sister for having kept her as a caregiver, as well as guilt for not having heard her mother calling on the night of her death. Eleanor is the first guest to arrive at Hill House, a manor that she finds hideous right after being admitted by the unwelcoming caretakers, who warn the party that they have to lock the gates when they leave after dark.

The group is light-hearted during their first day at Hill House. After a few hours in the house, Eleanor feels a sense of belonging somewhere for the first time, and the joy of having friends. That evening Dr. Montague tells them the history of Hill House. The house had been built eighty years ago by Mr Hugh Crain in the hope of raising his children and grandchildren in a comfortable country house. However, Crain loses his wife in a carriage accident soon before moving in. Left with two little girls, Crain remarries, but loses his second wife to a fall. His third wife dies in Europe of consumption, after which Crain closes down the house, never to return. Dr Montague mentions a couple deaths of dwellers on the premises along the decades, making it clear that none were related to murder or the paranormal. In spite of this, every person who had attempted to live in Hill House had left prematurely, refusing to give any account of the reasons.

The first night in Hill House is peaceful, and they all awake refreshed and ready to explore the building. They find the structure of the house remarkably odd: the design seems to revolve around circular motifs and it lacks straight angles, which could account for all the doors shutting on their own and the sense of disorientation of the occupants. The most striking room in the house seems to be the nursery: two grinning heads guard the entrance over the doorway, and in the spot where the gaze of the carvings meet, the temperature drops to unexplainable freezing levels. The library also appears somewhat extraordinary in construction, being a tower strangely attached to the main structure of the house. For reasons they cannot understand, Eleanor cannot bring herself to walk into the library.

The second night brings the first supernatural event. A very loud pounding sound on the doors awakens the two women in their connecting bedrooms, while the two men had been driven outside by a stray animal. The pounding sweeps the house in search of the women and violently bangs the locked door when it finds their room. After babbling in indefinable voices, the manifestation stops. When the men return, they have not heard anything unusual apart from the screams of the girls.

Hill House gradually targets (and disintegrates) Eleanor's initial autonomy. On the morning of the third day, the house singles out Eleanor by manifesting chalk writing on the wall that reads: 'help Eleanor come home.' Although this night is spent peacefully, the next day Theodora discovers her room and all her clothes smeared with blood, and a writing above her own bed with the similar inscription 'help Eleanor come home Eleanor.' That night, as they sleep in the same bedroom, Eleanor wakes up to the indefinable voices, first babbling, then laughing. Holding hands in the darkness, the two women experience how the temperature of the room decreases as the babbling becomes a child's cry for help and a shriek. Eleanor then confronts the house in rage and the lights go on. She is astounded to discover that Theodora had been asleep all along at too far a distance to have been holding her hand.

As Eleanor's illusions of independence and sense of belonging in the group crack, the house takes the opportunity to absorb her, making her grow increasingly lonely, torn between horror and attraction to the house. On an evening walk, the two women witness a ghostly picnic while they are followed by a terrifying presence in the garden that is never described. All these supernatural episodes test Eleanor's fragile self-reliance, feeding always on Eleanor's lack of a home or family affection.

The arrival of Mrs. Montague and her male assistant entertains the group for the next day. While these last two characters are to be ignored by Hill House, the initial group endures a severe evening of manifestations in which a pounding presence stalks the outside of their room and furniture falls as they feel the house rock and shake violently. It is at this point that Eleanor declares her intentions to give herself up to the house.

On the final night, the group is sitting together when Eleanor notices that she is the only one hearing footsteps and singing in the room. For the first time, instead of experiencing distress, she feels pride in being the one chosen by the house. Later on in the evening, Eleanor hears the voice of her mother calling, which triggers a frantic frenzy in her, running and laughing all over the building. When she reaches the library that used to terrify her, she enters, overtaken by feelings of having found home. She climbs up a rusty staircase known to be on the verge of collapsing, forcing an angry Luke to climb up to her rescue.

Fearing for her safety, Dr Montague insists she must leave. Eleanor, however, now envisions the house as her home, and refuses to go. After being forced into her car, she is killed when she crashes into a tree on the property. The book finishes with the same opening paragraph describing the insanity of Hill House, and how 'whatever walked there, walked alone.'

Jackson's book began as a writing exercise inspired by William Castle's film *The House on Haunted Hill* (1959), a standard haunted house story which stars Vincent Price and is a garish feast of violence. Jackson's story, however, has no violence, ghosts or demons, and yet it is highly effective and has been widely praised. Here we see an example of how greatly male and female treatments of the same material can vary.

Once initiated by Jackson, the trope of the evil house was pursued by both male and female writers. However, while male writers have praised and adopted the device, they persist in filling their narratives with extreme violence and satanic ritual. A brief survey of the best-selling haunted house narratives – Richard Matheson's *Hell House* (1971), Stephen King's *The Shining* (1977), and Jay Anson's *The Amityville Horror* (1977) – shows to what extent male authors rely on past evils, demons or the violation of burial grounds as possible explanations for the hauntings (as is the case with both King and Anson). This is equally valid for horror films by male directors, as we shall see below.

Just like *The Haunting of Hill House*, Richard Matheson's *Hell House* describes a scientific experiment that aims to prove the existence of the supernatural. It relies heavily on demonology, murder, torture, and sex crimes. This applies both to the past history of the building and to the narrative present.

A wealthy old man, close to the end of his life, finances a research experiment of a group of experts in the hope of proving the existence of an afterlife. The team is to stay for a week in a purportedly haunted building: Hell House, a manor built in 1919 by Emeric Belasco. For ten years, massacres including cannibalism, Satanism or necrophilia had been regularly held, until in 1929 police found everyone in the house dead except Belasco, who was never found. The research group includes Dr. Barrett, a sceptical old doctor, his wife Edith, the spiritualist Florence Tanner, and the only survivor of a former attempt to study the premises thirty years ago: the medium Benjamin F. Fisher.

Minor incidents such as locked front doors or a gramophone playing on its own begin almost on arrival. Soon, corpses are found and violence begins. Acts of sexual perversion and aggression follow one another. The spirits possess the minds of the researchers, murder both the doctor and the spiritualist, and are close to murdering the rest of the occupants on several occasions. As the book draws to an end, the deceased owner of the house is identified as responsible for the haunting. His remains are found in a sealed, hidden room covered in lead. Ultimately, the medium and the doctor's widow understand the secret torturing the ghost, based on fighting his own feelings of inadequacy by ongoing murdering. Fear in *Hell House* thus relies on graphic description rather than presenting the house as a character or as a claustrophobic structure. Its characters do not develop psychological attachments to the house and show no will to stay. Although the house is initially presented with a certain degree of sentience and as a participant in the manifestations, it is gradually revealed to be merely the location of crimes.

Similarly, Jay Anson's *The Amityville Horror*, which was originally presented by the Lutz family as purported true events, makes initial use of sentience, but as the story progresses the presence of the building weakens to allow room for other entities. The genesis of the story is taken from a true episode of a family massacre that occurred on the premises in 1974 when Ronnie DeFeo, aged 23, murdered his parents and younger siblings. Aware of the house's history, the buyers invite a priest to bless the house on the day they move. However, the priest is expelled from the house by an unseen voice, falling ill soon after at his rectory. Days later the five-year-old daughter befriends an invisible presence called Jodie, described by the girl as a pig with red eyes. The mother dreams recurrently of the murders and knows details about the massacre that she had not previously known. In addition, a secret sealed room covered in red is found in the basement. As the story unfolds, the reader finds episodes of levitation, direct sightings of ghosts and the pig-like creature, attacks, oozing of substances from the walls, animal sacrifices and references to a cursed Native American Indian cemetery, among other things. In consequence, while the Amityville house is initially presented as an evil place, the significance of setting, space and associated claustrophobia is minimal. As with Matheson, the house itself is not an antagonist but rather the location where other agents take action. In addition, the book does not rely on emotional attachments to the property. Rather, the occupants of the house only regard it as an investment and a place of residence.

Our last male author, Stephen King, has openly declared his admiration for Jackson's book, which he intended to emulate with *The Shining*. It should be pointed out that, sadly, the original story by Stephen King is to a great extent ignored by those who have not approached the book itself. While the film adaptations of Matheson's and Anson's films closely follow the original texts, this is not the case with *The Shining*, where much of the author's creative worth was discarded when taken to the big screen. In this story, the Overlook Hotel appears to be alive and aware, but its malignancy, it transpires, is the direct result of murders committed by members of the mafia and other criminals. King deploys graphic descriptions of these crimes and presents both sinful and innocent ghosts, as well as the animation of non-sentient matter such as the predatory trees in the hotel's topiary maze. However, the source of fear lies in the ominous surrendering of the protagonist to the ghosts' dictates to murder his own family. Once again, the author relies on bodily injury and physical aggression, and neglects any agency in the building, which once more proves to be just a setting.

I now turn to one of Jackson's leading female literary heirs, Anne Rivers Siddons. Nearly twenty years after Jackson, Siddons published *The House Next Door* (1978), which adopts similar techniques to those observed in 1959. Like its predecessor, Siddons relies on psychological dependence on the home. *The House Next Door* is the story of an intelligent, predatory house, for whose malevolence we are given no reasons at all – it is just evil. The narrative follows the consecutive habitations of three sets of occupants and their corresponding destruction – not necessarily through death. The story begins with the construction of a house in an idyllic spot – with no hint of it being built on a burial ground, and where no building had ever stood before. The completed structure is described as a charming modern house which earns the approval of everyone. However, one by one the house studies and destroys the lives of its occupants in unexpected ways.

The House Next Door is narrated by a mid-thirties, upper-middle class, married woman, Colquitt Kennedy. After an insight into the couple's pleasant existence, the story takes off with the disruption of their hedonistic suburban peace with the imminent development of their cherished adjacent section: a particularly charming spot with irregular terrain surrounded by trees with a brook nearby. When the Kennedys meet the young and novice architect Kim, they actually fall for the charms of the sketches of the modern house and even develop a close friendship with the architect.

The owners of the property are the Harralsons, a promising lawyer in a prestigious firm and his pregnant and pampered wife. Trouble starts soon before they move in, with the girl falling down the cellar stairs and miscarrying. Other strange incidents occur, such as dead bodies of animals being found near the back of the house. On the evening of the housewarming party, carefully planned to impress neighbours and colleagues, the celebration is shattered by unexpected events involving the death of the wife's father and a humiliating incident destroying her husband's position. The marriage is broken and the house is put up for sale. By the time the Harralsons sell the property Kim has begun to develop apprehensions regarding his creation.

The second occupants are the Sheehans. While the husband is warm and approachable, she conversely appears frail and absent. Colquitt learns about the loss of her father and brother in an airplane crash when she was a child, and the recent death of her only son when his helicopter crashed in Vietnam. The loss of their son drove the father to alcoholism and to take a mistress, all of which destroyed her mental equilibrium, keeping her in hospital with a catatonic seizure for several months. After her recovery, the couple bought the house next door in the hope of starting a new life. As with the Harralsons, it was the woman who fell in love with the house at first glance and insisted on moving there.

A strange episode disrupts the Sheehans's settling in their new home. One evening when she is alone in the house, the wife is severely shaken by watching a film in which a helicopter crashes during the Vietnam war. Although a neighbour corroborates having seen the film on their TV when dropping by on that night to check on the woman, no war film had been screened on TV on that evening. She is never informed of this confirmation of her paranormal experience, so she conveniently discards it as the fruit of her imagination. However, other incidents drive the woman back into catatonia for good. For instance, she receives phone calls from her dead son announcing that he is returning home, which again shatters her mental stability. During the Sheehans's tenancy, the Kennedys join Kim in believing that something is wrong with the house, the three admit having felt a strange, weird force at the property. The architect, tormented by the events for which he blames the evil, malignant house next door, leaves for Europe.

The last occupants are the Greenes. The father is presented as an unfriendly, abusive Jewish academic who has insecurity issues relating to his ethnicity. He patronises his wife and is harsh to the eight-year-old girl. As soon as the family moves in things begin to go wrong. The child starts to suffer from digestive disorders. The mother, in turn, appears disoriented and inefficient, losing her formerly good administrative skills. As time goes by, minor unexplainable incidents become increasingly frequent, such as strange failures in the power supply, bizarrely stained clothes or items breaking on their own. All these little incidents seem aimed to provoke outbursts of anger in the father, who becomes gradually abusive. On their last night, the father is particularly humiliating and cruel at a large party organised by the Greenes to impress the academic community. When only two of the neighbours attend, the mother is accused of not having sent the invitations, although she knows she had done so. On that evening, she kills both her husband and child and commits suicide.

The narrator is aware of all this, due to the proximity of her property but also as a result of warnings from the architect. After this accumulation of extraordinary episodes, the Kennedys decide to take action and contact the media to dissuade possible new buyers, but the new negative publicity causes the couple to lose their jobs and become obsessed in their crusade to destroy the evil house. In order to prevent further projects they murder the architect, who had recently returned from Europe. The book draws to an end as the Kennedys prepare to burn down the house, knowing that they will somehow be killed in the process. Their sacrifice proves useless since the book's epilogue depicts the original sketches of the house having survived its destruction. No character ever finds a reason why the building should be haunted, including its architect, who is presented as an innocent man that dies without understanding the source of the malignancy.

Both *The Haunting of Hill House* and *The House Next Door* have been adapted into films which offer further evidence of the different fears underlying male and female psyches. When male directors and screenwriters are in the process of adapting a female text for the screen, it would seem that their inherited understanding of what is to be feared in a house dictates the introduction of extreme violence, demonology or past crimes. Specifically, two of the three film adaptations shift the emphasis from the malignancy of the house to that of a particular character.

I will discuss the second film adaptation of *The Haunting of Hill House* first. In Jan de Bont's *The Haunting* (1999), Hugh Crain – the original and deceased owner of the house in the book – is revealed as the perpetrator of the haunting in a similar way to that in Matheson's *Hell House*. We witness the abuse of orphans, graphic decapitations, multiple ghosts, and a final confrontation between a devil-like Crain and Eleanor. In very much the same vein, Jeff Woolnough's made-for-TV film *The House Next Door* (2006) makes a devil-like architect responsible for the haunting. These male adaptations ignore the many and explicit references to the building's own awareness in the female originals.

The first adaptation of *The Haunting of Hill House*, Robert Wise's *The Haunting* (1963), might initially appear to disprove the theory being advanced in this chapter. Mr. Wise's film definitely cannot be accused of being untrue to

Jackson's focus on spatial restriction. The supernatural events in the novel are not depicted, and most of the action takes place inside the house to heighten the audience's feeling of claustrophobia. However, it should be remembered that Shirley Jackson herself supervised the script and the filming. In fact, when Nelson Gidding was preparing the script for the film, he came to believe that the novel was not a ghost story at all, but rather the jumbling together of the insane thoughts of Eleanor Vance.[14] Tellingly, a surprised Jackson told him that the novel was definitely about the supernatural.[15]

As can be seen, male authors and directors systematically prioritise fear of the *Other* over the *house* itself. The fact that they are generally reluctant – to say the least – to privilege an inexplicably malevolent house over graphic violence and external explanations for the haunted house's malevolence, coupled with the fact that the evil house originated with Jackson's *The Haunting of Hill House*, would seem to support the theory that females have inherited a gender-conditioned ability to see a fearful side of the house itself, which goes someway to explaining the limited male mastery of the possibilities of the evil house narrative.

Notes

[1] Isaac Marks, 'Innate and Learned Fears Are at Opposite Ends of a Continuum of Associability,' *Behaviour Research and Therapy* 40 (2002): 165.

[2] Ibid., 167.

[3] Gleb Shumyatsky, et al., 'Stathmin, a Gene Enriched in the Amygdala, Controls Both Learned and Innate Fear,' *Cell* 123 (2005): 697-709.

[4] Isaac Marks, 'Innate and Learned Fears,' 165.

[5] Arne Öhman and Susan Mineka, 'The Malicious Serpent: Snakes as a Prototypical Stimulus for an Evolved Module of Fear', *Current Directions in Psychological Science* 12 (2003): 6.

[6] Ibid., 7.

[7] David H. Rakison, 'Does Women's Greater Fear of Snakes and Spiders Originate in Infancy?' *Evolution and Human Behavior* 30 (2009): 442.

[8] Ibid., 442.

[9] Ibid., 442.

[10] Mats Fredrikson et al., 'Gender and Age Differences in the Prevalence of Specific Fears and Phobias. *Behaviour Research and Therapy* 34 (1996): 37.

[11] Ibid.

[12] Rutgers University, 'Mice Missing "Fear" Gene Slow to Protect Offspring', *ScienceDaily* website, viewed on 20 May 2014, http://www.sciencedaily.com/releases/2008/09/080915174548.htm.

[13] Catalin Ghita, in this volume.

[14] Tom Weaver, *I Was a Monster Movie Maker: Conversations with 22 SF and Horror Filmmakers* (Jefferson, NC: McFarland & Co, 2001), 64.
[15] Ibid., 64-65.

Bibliography

Anson, Jay. *The Amityville Horror.* London: Pan, 1978.

Couture, Suzette. *The House Next Door.* Directed by Jeff Woolnough. Montreal: Muse Entertainment, 2006.

Fredrikson, Mats, Peter Annas, Hakan Fisher and Gustav Wik, 'Gender and Age Differences in the Prevalence of Specific Fears and Phobias.' *Behaviour Research and Therapy* 34.1 (1996): 33-39.

Jackson, Shirley. *The Haunting of Hill House.* London: Robinson, 1999 [1959].

King, Stephen. *The Shining.* London: New English Library, 1982 [1977].

Knight, Denise D., ed. *'The Yellow Wall-Paper' and Selected Stories of Charlotte Perkins Gilman.* Newark: University of Delaware Press, 1994.

Marks, Isaac. 'Innate and Learned Fears are at Opposite Ends of a Continuum of Associability.' *Behaviour Research and Therapy* 40 (2002): 165-67.

Matheson, Richard. *Hell House.* New York: Viking, 1971.

Öhman, Arne, and Susan Mineka, 'The Malicious Serpent: Snakes as a Prototypical Stimulus for and Evolved Module of Fear.' *Current Directions in Psychological Science* 12 (2003): 5-9.

Peattie, Elia Wilkinson. *The Shape of Fear and Other Ghostly Tales.* Freeport, NY: Books for Libraries, 1969 [1898].

Self, David, and Michael Tolkin. *The Haunting.* Directed by Jan de Bont. Universal City, CA: DreamWorks Pictures, 1999.

Shumyatsky, Gleb, Gaël Malleret, Ryong-Moon Shin, Shuichi Takizawa, Keith Tully, Evgeny Tsvetkov, Stanislav S. Zakharenko, Jamie Joseph, Svetlana Vronskaya, DeQi Yin, Ulrich K. Schubart, Eric R. Kandel and Vadim Y. Bolshakov, 'Stathmin, a Gene Enriched in the Amygdala, Controls both Learned and Innate Fear.' *Cell* 123, (2005): 697-709.

Siddons, Anne Rivers. *The House Next Door.* New York: Ballantine, 1983 [1978].

Rakison, David H. 'Does Women's Greater Fear of Snakes and Spiders Originate in Infancy?' *Evolution and Human Behavior* 30 (2009): 438-44.

Weaver, Tom. *I Was a Monster Movie Maker: Conversations with 22 SF and Horror Filmmakers.* Jefferson, NC: McFarland & Co, 2001.

Wharton, Edith. *The Ghost Stories of Edith Wharton.* London: Virago, 1996 [1910].

White, Robb. *The House on Haunted Hill.* Directed by William Castle. Hacienda Heights, CA: Allied Artists, 1959.

Clara Pallejá-López is a lecturer at the Catholic University of Murcia, Spain. While interested in fantasy in Spanish and English film and fiction, currently her research is focused on the transmission of genetic fears and the way in which these determine the construction of meaning in literature.

Commitment to Self: What Language Reveals about Male Fear of Commitment

Izabela Dixon and Magdalena Hodalska

Abstract
Much has been said and written in the Western world about gender differences, which involve many, if not most, everyday domains. Metaphorically, the distance between the sexes can be measured in astronomical terms: women are supposedly from Venus, while men are apparently from Mars. However, looking at the issue in a more down-to-earth manner, perhaps in time the rift may become smaller, particularly because women seem to have toughened up (at least their image) and, with every passing year, more and more men lean towards metrosexuality. However, are these changes affecting people's mind-sets sufficiently to effect a departure from the well-embedded schematic views of each other? Among the questions that the authors aim to raise in this brief study are those concerning communication issues and emotional interaction between the sexes. Central to this study is what occurs when male sensitivity and courage are put to the test by their partners in the context of relationships and commitment. Various communication strategies men commonly apply when challenged by situations which require empathic responses will be considered as well as communication blunders resulting from the metaphorical euphemisms men use in their attempts to conceal their deficient emotional maturity. To address these issues the study will draw on such disciplines as linguistics, cognitive linguistics, media and cultural studies, sociology and psychoanalysis. While as distant planets men and women follow their own orbits, they do occasionally seem to be on collision course or even collide. Often these collisions cause ruptures and explosions of supernova proportions.

Key Words: Men, language of emotions, commitment, anxiety, fears, emotional sensitivity.

*****

1. From Happiness and Love to Fear and Insecurity

There is no denying that happiness, being intimately related to such states as harmony, balance, safety and satisfaction, is something that lies at the source of people's well-being. Love is also a source of happiness, as is a fulfilling relationship. However, in their attempts to find happiness and love, many people tend to pursue what gives them physical and physiological fulfilment, contentment and comfort. This is hardly surprising since material goods bring constant gratification while happiness, the definition of which has evaded both western and eastern philosophers, is elusive. This also applies to love.

Love is an abstract concept which, according to many, is becoming even more abstract as increasingly it is something people mostly read about or see enacted at the cinema or on the TV screen. Perhaps it is an exaggeration to suggest that love is crossing over into the domains of fantasy or fiction, but romantic encounters among the now more independent and sometimes somewhat masculine women and more feminine men pose a number of problems. For a variety of reasons, people do, however, enter into relationships seeking comfort, warmth and security.

The change in the long-established paradigm of male dominance seems to be causing a degree of confusion resulting not so much in gender equality as in a gradual role reversal. Many feminists would argue that, at least temporarily, the balance needs to be tipped in women's favour to counteract some of the effects of the previous influential paradigm, but the consequence is a notable identity crisis causing fear and estrangement on many levels of existence including cross-gender interaction.

Currently, the institution of marriage is failing and the newly formed legal partnerships are not very stable. However, being single is no longer a matter of choice only. More and more frequently it is a consequence of limited availability of compatible partners. Furthermore, many people declare a fear of starting a relationship, associating such a bond with something restrictive, confining and thus undesirable. Love and commitment are seemingly frightening. To Žižek, for example, 'falling in love' is 'terrible' or 'traumatic'[1] as is the very idea of *falling*. With regard to marriage, Žižek suggests that love is redundant in this configuration: 'Rather' he says, 'we look for better characteristics and economic backgrounds' all due to what he calls 'narcissistic economy.'[2]

Sukran Karatas, the author of a text in this volume entitled 'Scientific Explanations of Fear and Anxiety,' focuses on the choice of Deity which is integral to the process of attaining a total equilibrium leading to peace, happiness and a fear-free existence. Karatas notes that '[e]strangement is one of the biggest causes of fear and anxiety in the 21st century.'[3] The reading of her text offers insight into the spiritual state of people living their lives from a first person singular perspective, claiming SELF as the centre of their individual universe. This solipsistic universe results in self-indulgence and remoteness. Estrangement is also typical of 'social isolation' and such feelings as 'vulnerability and the heightened sense of being at risk' from the other.[4] These characteristics of modern existence are also discussed by other social philosophers, including Bauman[5], Svendsen[6] and Glassner.[7]

Regardless of the newly advertised cosmopolitan trends in female-male relationships, which are by no means based on love and romance, even the strongest and most independent women are often sensitive and romantically disposed. Such women tend to have many expectations of their potential life partners wanting them to be empathic, attentive and loving. According to them, modern men should not be strangers to the products of the fashion industry, but at the same time, they should remain manly, virile and preferably chivalrous. On the other hand, while many modern men tend to conform to certain of the obligations of the new paradigm, such as embracing metrosexuality and their more effeminate side, they nevertheless find it hard to relinquish the desire to be in control, which helps them to hold on to their culturally-induced sense of masculinity.

2. Men, Emotions and Fear of Commitment

Emotions are universal to humanity, biological in origin, physiological in nature, and, what is more, they are culture- and context-bound.[8] Emotional states are an inescapable part of each human being and yet some people expend much of their vital energy fighting, what some see as largely disruptive episodes.[9] Love, becomes thus one of these disruptive forces:

> Everyone knows love is the greatest thing, but at the same time, it is the most horrible thing. Can you imagine yourself living a nice life and meeting with friends and having one-night-stands, but all of a sudden, you *fall* passionately *in love*? *It's horrible. It ruins your whole life. We are afraid of that.* [...] Even love, passionate love, is too dangerous.[10]

Žižek's noticeably male perspective, italicised above, is particularly relevant to the aims of this chapter, the focus of which is men's fear of commitment. Love, as Žižek suggests, is a dreaded and dangerous emotion. A natural reaction to fear is to recoil and retreat; not surprisingly, then, many modern men, who are no longer characterised by such outdated qualities as chivalry and prowess, take evasive action if expected to commit romantically to another person.

Undoubtedly, to a degree, both genders have reservations concerning being in a regular relationship, fearing love. Such fear, however, is likely to have somewhat divergent sources and manifestations. What perhaps affects both men and women is the fragile nature of self-esteem which, in the context of relationships, is usually at considerable risk. The difference is that for men, according to the still-functioning social paradigms, damage to self-esteem may be more socially harmful as it threatens what remains of their masculinity. Since emotions may unmask the seemingly strongest of people, for men this makes emotions socially dangerous and undesirable, as pointed out by Galasiński:

> Emotions are seen as unintended and uncontrollable: they are dangerous and render people vulnerable. They are physical and natural, and thus in opposition to civilisation. [...] [T]oday's Western outlook on emotions is more negative than positive. While we may like having emotions, we do not want to lose

control over our actions or bodies. But if you want to stay in
control, and men – at least stereotypically – are thought to want it
more than anything, emotionality cannot be good for them. Men
cannot be emotional; *men don't cry* is a saying that has versions
in different languages across Europe.[11]

This view is confirmed by the cognitive linguistic studies of concepts related to
emotions, among the aims of which is to construct linguistically encoded and
entrenched models. On a conceptual level, emotions are ascribed many of the
characteristics of such negative concepts as forces (physical, mental, natural),
insanity, illness or opponents.[12] As a result of social expectations, rules of conduct
and a CONTROL IS UP schema,[13] control of emotions is desirable, particularly for
men as is noted by the author of the above quotation. While susceptibility to carnal
desires is acceptable, emotional vulnerability is not. Hence, while men quite
readily 'jump' into women's beds, they are considerably less ready to take the
'plunge' and declare that they are actually in a relationship.

Long-term relationships are viewed with caution. Perhaps this is partly because
in the Western world the institution of marriage has been in crisis for a number of
decades now, and, analogically, long-term relationships are viewed as confining
and virtually anachronistic – basically prison-like – a notion which may be
compared to the MARRIAGE IS A PRISON conceptual metaphor.[14] It seems that
Cosmo style flings and one-night stands are in vogue.[15] There are several possible
reasons for this.

In the view of psychologists[16] and social philosophers, one of the most palpable
reasons for the flight from commitment is personality disorders or personality
crises. Žižek notes: 'Today we have an extremely narcissistic notion of
personality.'[17] In a commodity-driven world, people are encouraged to live inward-
looking, not to say, self-obsessed lifestyles dominated by the pronouns 'I', 'me',
and 'myself', the last preferably being prefixed with 'for' – 'for myself.' This
problem is compounded by the fact that anything that would require effort,
sacrifice, responsibility, compromise, devotion, and, significantly, coping with
uncomfortable feelings, could diminish the 'I' and spoil the harmony of living
solely 'with', 'by', and 'for' oneself. In other words men fear having to leave their
comfort zone as this inevitably entails loss of personal freedom. This common
anxiety involves a number of 'ifs' partly resulting from the necessary shift in the
basic day-to-day paradigm from 'care free' to 'responsible' or from 'casual' to
'committed.' This may also mean having to exchange something basically
undemanding, like casual sex, for something that is potentially devoid of the 'fun
factor.' Casual relationships may be experienced as adventure, while committed
relationships tend to be associated with drab reality, drudgery and effort.

Fear of commitment, or one of its forms – marriage – is expressed in a poem by Walter McDonald (1998) in which the poet established analogies between two seemingly distant domains: the institution of marriage and an adrenaline sport:

> Marriage is a bungee jump off some box canyon in Colorado (...) The ropes felt new enough and he swore he measured them, the fall to the rocks (...). We heard a match strike, the sizzle of hemp. We checked the ropes, the stiff knots tied by someone who flunked that lesson in scouts.[18]

Through six stanzas the poet draws a number of metaphorical mappings which indicate the risks people take when they decide to 'take the plunge' and marry. Such lexemes as *rope, hemp* and *knot* are thematically associated with bungee jumping, while metaphorically they may stand for safety and 'tying the knot' – an idiomatic expression synonymous with marriage. The sense of doubt and uncertainty in the poem is also conveyed by reference to the poor credentials of the registrar, or the rocks against which the plunging couple may crash.

It would not be much of an exaggeration to say that declarations of undying love are basically reserved for cliché-ridden romantic stories or films. In real life they are rare, especially from contemporary male suitors. It is a well-known, though anecdotal, fact that the best moment to get a man to agree to the proverbial 'anything' (such as marriage) is at the moment of his high arousal, namely, immediately before 'coitus.' This has frequently been mocked in a variety of genres, such as comedy series and the acts of stand-up comedians. The same principle may be applied to the declaration of 'I love you.' Similarly, if such questions as: 'Do you love me? Do you care about me? Are we in a relationship?' are asked at the wrong time, the results may be catastrophic or, at least, very unpleasant to the one making the enquiry. Some of the women whose experiences are reported in this chapter experienced psychologically painful consequences. At other times, when some form of communication has taken place, the hastily uttered declarations are soon reconsidered and counteracted with 'I don't know what made me say this, or even: You make me say things that I don't mean!' Fully aware of the power of emotions that force men to say 'things that they don't mean', the authors of this chapter see the language of emotions as serving different discursive purposes from the recipient's and the speaker's points of view.[19] Interestingly, with regard to the study of the language of emotions, Fiehler states:

> Although there have been a series of attempts to develop [...] theories to include emotionality [...], these theories at their core and in their fundamental assumptions do not provide for emotionality.[20]

Language, however passionate or dispassionate, reflects the particular psychological condition of the people involved in emotional exchanges. The effects of such can be studied from both the speaker's and also the recipient's/interpreter's point of view. It is the latter of the two that has become the focus of the present study.

3. The Language of Emotions: Evasive 'Man---oeuvres'[21]

Central to this study are sample utterances the emotive communicative potential and semantic message of which are assessed on the basis of interdisciplinary tools from such fields as cognitive linguistics, involving image and concept schemas and conceptual metaphor (CM) theory, socio-cultural (gender) theories and aspects of psychology. From the socio-economic point of view the women whose experiences are presented, as well as the men whose utterances are reported, are well-educated and middle-class and represented by predominantly professional groups (lawyers, academics, doctors). Their ages range from mid-thirties to mid-forties.

Although, it is not our purpose to speculate as to the existence of possible psychological disorders in the men whose utterances are analysed, certain conjectures may be made on the basis of style, which may suggest that some speakers could be classified as Pathological Narcissists, Peter Pans, Don Juans,[22] Hysterics[23] or play-actors of the histrionic type.[24] Moreover, we cannot dismiss the fact that the men in question might suffer from various psychopathologies[25] such as paranoid/schizoid[26] condition or other personality malfunctions,[27] such as antisocial,[28] obsessive-compulsive, avoidant personality, or dependent personality[29] disorder.

However, having presumed that there is no such thing as normality, since, as psychotherapists argue, there are only diagnosed patients and not-yet-diagnosed ones, it is the utterances in their contexts that are the focus of our study. On the strength of the linguistic data, we propose different categories of strategies which men adopt to express their lack of commitment, care or involvement or their desire to escape from their responsibilities as partners, husbands or fathers.

Furthermore, from an assessment of the emotional content of the utterances, schematic models will be abstracted. The connection between language and emotions is far more than tentative, particularly because language, among other roles, also performs an emotive function: as Bamberg points out, 'language and emotion are two concurrent, parallel systems in use, and their relationship exists in that one system (emotions) impacts on the performance of the other (language).[30] Bamberg also suggests that while language may be viewed as affording direct access to how emotions are conceptualised it may also serve as an intermediary in the process of understanding what emotions *are*.[31] The juxtaposition of *emotional women* and *unemotional men* in this text is not intentional and should not be seen as valid. We merely seek to stress that the emotional impact of certain statements confirms the firmly embedded folk schema that WORDS HAVE THE POWER TO WOUND.

In his work *Men and the Language of Emotions* Dariusz Galasiński explores two super-strategies preferred by men which are: speaking directly and distancing.[32] These strategies, as Galasiński maintains, are the means by which men establish the dominant model of masculinity, while 'distancing offers a strategy to maintain the pretence of meeting the requirements of the dominant model of masculinity.'[33] The latter strategy is also used to distance the speakers from emotions within their relationships and their emotions towards the Other[34] (=Woman[35]). Men tend to refer to their relationships by using terms such as: 'I have/had a close relationship' rather than employing language expressive of commitment, such as 'My beloved wife.'[36]

4. Communicating Fear

Our study is partly discourse driven and partly a case study. The linguistic data was derived from interviews conducted with women who recounted experiences which they described as 'painful, sad, or devastating' and which were caused by particular male utterances under specific circumstances. From each account presented in the study we have attempted to abstract a linguistic-behavioural strategy with, where possible, a corresponding schematic model.

4.1. Emotional Distance

The ways in which people react to various life situations can be studied at, among others, behavioural, psychological, biological, cultural, socio-anthropological, and (para)linguistic levels. In terms of the cognitive sciences, reactions, behaviours, states and perceptions are mentally encoded and schematised. One of the conceptual schemas relating to social situations is CONTROL, as in BEING IN CONTROL of one's life.

> **Situation 1:**
> Having broken up with his long-term partner, the man asks her if she knows a good cardiologist. In case she does not, he offers some assistance. (Later, responding to what she has taken for sarcasm, she recommends a good psychiatrist).

The first situation demonstrates how the man is trying to remain in control of a particular situation by assuming a seemingly protective role. Governed by a MAN IN CONTROL schema, under the pretence of offering caring advice, which to the recipient sounds insensitive or even sarcastic, the speaker asks if his recipient needs help finding a good cardiac specialist. By this proposal the man creates the illusion concern for the person he has just hurt. It seems that a heart specialist might undo or reduce the emotional damage the man feels responsible for having caused.

4.2. Emotional Detachment and Indifference

Emotional disengagement is a psychological coping strategy which may have social implications. People who employ this strategy tend to avoid admitting to a problem which would otherwise cause them some emotional distress. This strategy usually includes both the mental and physical planes. The mental plane involves the act of conscious or subconscious suppression, while the physical plane involves avoiding exposure to socially uncomfortable situations which could bring about negative feelings. In other words, attempting to evade their feelings of guilt, shame or inadequacy, agents position themselves outside the uncomfortable zone thus putting a distance between themselves and the source of discomfort. This behaviour has different schematic representations such as: VAGUENESS, DEFERMENT/POSTPONEMENT and EVASION.

The VAGUENESS schema does not result from the speaker's lack of communicative skills; on the contrary, it may signify deliberate avoidance of an emotional declaration. The perlocutionary effect of a vague message may have a negligible impact on the recipient, passing almost unnoticed and thus gaining the speaker some time. It may, however, produce a negative effect as vagueness may be understood for what it is – a lack of decisive feelings on the speaker's part.

There is little difference between VAGUENESS and POSTPONEMENT as they can both be understood in terms of temporal effects (see Situation 2). POSTPONEMENT is a classic fear of commitment strategy. In Situation 2, the semi-declaration 'You know what I feel' is deceptive. 'Vagueness introduces the presence of uncertainty of meaning.'[37] Fear of commitment leads to deception.[38]

Situation 2:
Having been asked repeatedly about his feelings the man keeps saying, "You know what I feel; I'll tell you later". A few years later, having been finally persuaded to address the question, the man replies "I don't know what I feel".

Situation 3 is indicative of a DEFERMENT strategy, which links with the GOOD/BAD TIME or THERE AND THEN schema. As in Situation 2, the speaker refrains from addressing a problem immediately, thus allowing himself to remain within his comfort zone. A business-like response gives the man some semblance of control, indicating that this is not a GOOD MOMENT/TIME for him to address the question.

Situation 3:
A woman calls her partner to tell him about an accident she had which may result in an operation. Hearing about the potential seriousness of her condition, the man says: "Call me on Friday, after 5 p.m.".

By adding time to the physical distance, the message is interpreted by the recipient as a series of other possible statements: 'Go and talk to somebody else. It's not my problem. I may be ready to deal with it on Friday afternoon when the weekend starts.' All of these suggest that the man is incapable of an empathic response when this is most needed. By DEFERMENT the man may have a sense of being in CONTROL, allocating himself a time limit for decisions concerning his commitment to this relationship. Deferment is often indicative of stress and fear of having to cope with a difficult situation. The man also focuses on SELF, as in 'I AM important – You are NOT.'

The next situation is an example of EVASION – or escaping from a disagreeable situation by DISENGAGEMENT. In Situation 4, the *tram* as a means of transport also becomes a metaphorical VEHICLE FOR SAFETY which enables the man to put physical distance between himself and an emotionally uncomfortable situation. The haste of retreat may be indicative of a feeling of guilt, uncomfortable feelings being best disposed of quickly:

Situation 4:
A man leaves his pregnant wife for another woman. A few years later they accidently meet on the street, where an emotional exchange takes place. The woman, who has been raising the child as a single mother, has for the first time an opportunity to confront the man with what he subjected her to. The woman reported that during her emotional outburst when she was telling the man that he destroyed everything, he cut her off saying "Yeah, yeah, I know, It was nice to see you, but I must go. I have a tram to catch". This incident took place in Cracow, where trams come every three minutes.

Situation 5 is a variant of the EVASION strategy and also demonstrates INDIFFERENCE in the way both men stay detached from what would otherwise be regarded as an emotional situation:

Situation 5a:
A pregnant wife asks her husband if he will drive her to hospital when labour starts. To this the husband responds: "Well, why? Take a taxi!".

Situation 5b:
A different husband, when asked for the same assistance, says:
"The emergency room is right around the corner!".

Both men show aloofness. In Situation 5a, the man may see taking a taxi as legitimate and justifiable, but in fact he is clearly distancing himself from his responsibility, transferring it onto others, such as, in this case, a taxi driver, hospital staff and the wife herself. The women who experienced Situation 5, however, interpreted the comments as those of men trying to extricate themselves from what they perceived as a potentially difficult situation, thus displaying callousness and possibly fear.

4.3. Role Reversal
In male dominant societies women are often portrayed as the fair or weak sex while at the same time they are expected to take care of the home and children and also deal with everyday life situations, all these requiring considerable amounts of physical and mental stamina. It could be argued that having to organise and navigate through a wide range of daily activities, women have developed various coping strategies, which would account for their strength and determination. However, traditionally, it was men rather than women who went to war, defeated enemies and killed dragons to protect the weak.

Modern fiction tries abolish such images creating female superheroes or superheroines, among whom may be listed: Wonder Woman, Lara Croft and, more recently, Mockingjay in *The Hunger Games*[39] and Tris in *Divergent*.[40] In an increasing number of TV shows and series, men are being portrayed as the sensitive ones, while women are strong, down-to-earth types. This is well illustrated in the popular comedy series *The Big Bang Theory*.[41] It could therefore be said that female weakness in the past was perhaps given too much emphasis, while male sensitivity has always been understated. In fact, both genders have always had the capacity to be strong and sensitive, depending on personality and circumstances, as demonstrated in the following situations.

Situation 6:
A divorced woman receives regular phone calls from her ex-husband with regard to their daughter over whom she has been granted custody. During one of the routine phone calls, and in response to a question about their daughter's health, the woman felt the need to explain to her ex-husband that the child might actually have a serious medical condition "You know she's having problems with her kidneys. We saw a nephrologist last week. The doctor said something about a kidney transplant..."

> Interrupting her, the girl's father abruptly says: "No, no, no! I
> was asking about her cold, her runny nose, you know".

This particular communicative act shows that the caller had a clear goal concerning the exchange of information, but only within a very specific frame of reference. The situational goal for the man was to perform a routine task and to be told exactly what he wanted to hear, which, in this case, was the answer to his question. This leads to the conjecture that the man had possibly anticipated a simple and trouble-free answer. This would be supported by his insistence, which schematically may be interpreted as a STICK TO THE POINT subschema, subordinate to the EXACTNESS schema. With regard to the emotional content of this exchange, it may be suggested that the speaker was not ready to engage in the emotional burden he was being loaded with. His disregard for the more serious condition is a way of wanting something easier to deal with, which may translate to: 'I was asking for a lighter load. You can deal with the heavier one.' The seeming lack of concern may be indicative of fear and the inability of the man to address his unmanly helplessness. In this case, the woman is required to be the emotionally strong one.

The next situation comes under an OBLIGATION schema which governs a range of behaviours that are to be expected in particular situations. The expectation of fulfilment, or at least an appropriate response to a specific obligation, indicates that the schema has a strong sociological motivation. The situation demonstrates that when a person feels unable to perform an obligation, he or she may ask to be released from the duty. The speaker, however, expects more than just casual relief; rather, he seems to want his wife to respect his *sensitivity*:

Situation 7:
> A woman who has been hospitalised, asks her husband in a
> telephone conversation whether he could come and visit her, to
> which he says "I can't visit you in hospital; you know the smell
> makes me sick".

The woman expected something different, as is evidenced by what she said in her interview for the purpose of this study: 'Of course, I knew how he felt about hospitals, but I thought that he would visit me anyway... do the right thing, you know.' Expecting her husband to come, the wife clearly wanted to feel cared for. She pointed out that under certain conditions people overcome 'their whimsical tendencies and act up rather than down.' The interviewee's husband's defensive refusal is symptomatic of his inability to show compassion while at the same time having compassion for himself.[42] Embracing his weakness, the man in Situation 7 reveals his deficient masculine nature. While fear of hospitals is very common, the man's behaviour sends a very negative emotional message to his wife, which is expressive both of this fear and the limited nature of his commitment.

Situation 8 is an illustration of the complete reversal of masculine and feminine cultural archetypes, as it was the case in the example given by Galasiński pointing out, 'It is women who can be real hunters,'[43] probably because they are capable of dealing with aggressive beasts or, in this case, Rottweilers running loose in a front garden:

Situation 8:
A man afraid of his own dogs running in the garden tells his wife: "You go and catch the dogs, dear, I'll wait here".

With regard to this role reversal, Galasiński states: 'The stereotypical and academic models of masculinity have been dismissed in one move. The helpless men are juxtaposed with practical women who manage to survive in the urban jungle.' The man in Situation 8 encourages his wife to go ahead of him and clear the way. This request for a safe passage indicates that the woman is more in control of the aggressive animals than her husband and becomes the pack leader.

In his book, Galasiński reports on how women perceive their unemployed husbands: 'Men cry, men break down; they have no spine, no character. It is the woman who seems to be the foundation upon which the weakling man can lean.'[44] While Situation 8 is not entirely parallel with the case studied by Galasiński,[45] it is analogous because it shows a man in a vulnerable position. Clearly, in this situation it is the woman who wears the proverbial *trousers* in the family.

5. Committed to Fear

Fear of commitment in relationships – be they formal or informal, long-lasting or short-term – has been the focus of this brief study. It is not our aim to claim that romantic love does not exist or that all men are 'emotionally autistic.'[46] The observations that we are making merely suggest that fear of relationships has increased in recent decades and that men have started to hide in their metaphorical shells.

In his book *Unreasonable Men* Victor J. Seidler remarks:

But if we never learn to share our feelings with those we are close to, thinking of this as a form of 'self-indulgence' that might be expected of women but is inexcusable for men, then we never really learn to *share* ourselves. And it is true that as men we are constantly holding ourselves back even from those with whom we are most intimate.[47]

Various personality dysfunctions seem to be on the rise in the contemporary world probably due to the general state of confusion people experience when the new paradigms have not yet been firmly established and the old ones have not fallen into disuse. The paradigm in which marriage is still a desirable social institution has not entirely lost its validity, but it is in crisis. The new paradigm promoted by the media and the capitalist economy stresses 'I' as being central to everyone's world. This new 'universal' order has made people more egotistic and self-seeking. Instant gratification and intolerance of uncomfortable feelings, which are best swept away or not addressed, or which are projected onto other people, seem integral to people's mental peace, which has little to do with happiness. Men, at least those whose utterances have been analysed, seem particularly prone to indulge in this newly evolved paradigm.

One of the underlying problems highlighted in the present chapter is men's difficulty in relating to their own emotions and their reluctance to show appropriate levels of empathy towards women. Men's fear of commitment may have many roots, and these may stem from childhood experiences, traditional gender roles, social expectations and changing realities. The problem may also be one of communication. Refering to Locke, von Humbolt, Heidegger, Sapir, Worf, Quine and Derrida, Hejwowski suggests that 'the impossibility of communication between people [results] from excessive and unrealistic expectations. Human communicative needs are so varied that communication must resemble a complicated game based on foreseeing and inferring.'[48] Does this mean, then, that there is little hope for men and women to come close enough without the danger of meteorite-like showers of insensitive remarks? Probably, yes. Sometimes hope is all that remains.

Notes

[1] Slavoj Žižek, *Demanding the Impossible* (Cambridge: Polity Press, 2013), 81.
[2] Žižek, *Demanding the Impossible*, 82.
[3] Sukran Karatas, in this volume.
[4] Frank Furedi, *Culture of Fear Revisited: Risk-Taking and the Morality of Low Expectation* (London: Continuum, 2009), 135.
[5] Zygmunt Bauman, *Liquid Fear* (Cambridge: Polity Press, 2008).
[6] Lars Svendsen, *Philosophy of Fear* (London: Reaktion Books, 2008).
[7] Barry Glassner, *The Culture of Fear: Why Americans Are Afraid of the Wrong Things* (New York: Basic Books, 1999).
[8] Dariusz Galasiński, *Men and the Language of Emotions* (New York: Palgrave Macmilan, 2004), 3.
[9] Anna Wierzbicka, *Emotions across Languages and Cultures* (Cambridge: Cambridge University Press, 1999), 20.

[10] Žižek, *Demanding the Impossible*, 83.

[11] Galasiński, *Men and Language*, 12.

[12] Zoltán Kövecses, *Metaphor and Emotion: Language, Culture, and Body in Human Feeling* (Cambridge: Cambridge University Press, 2007).

[13] George Lakoff and Mark Johnson, *Metaphors We Live By* (Chicago, London: The University of Chicago Press, 2003), 17.

[14] Kövecses, *Metaphor and Emotion*, 111.

[15] Žižek, *Demanding the Impossible*, 83.

[16] Otto F. Kernberg, 'Pathological Narcissism and Narcissistic Personality Disorder: Theoretical Background and Diagnostic Classification,' in *Disorders of Narcissism: Diagnostic, Clinical and Empirical Implications*, ed. Elsa F. Ronningstam (Washington: American Psychiatric Press, 1998), 29-51; Heinz Kohut, *The Analysis of the Self: A Systematic Approach to the Psychoanalitic Treatment of Narcissistic Personality Disorders* (NY: International Universities Press, 1971); David Shapiro, *Neurotic Styles* (NY: Basic Books, 1965); Glen O. Gabbard, *Psychodynamic Psychiatry in Clinical Practice* (Washington: American Psychiatric Publishing, 2005).

[17] Žižek, *Demanding the Impossible*, 85.

[18] Walter McDonald, *Marriage is a Bungee Jump, The Writers Almanac with Garrison Keillor* web site. Viewed 1 February 2015.
http://writersalmanac.publicradio.org/index.php?date=2011/11/02

[19] Galasiński, *Men and Language*, 5.

[20] Reinhard Fiehler, 'How to Do Emotions with Words: Emotionality in Conversations,' in *The Verbal Communication of Emotions: Interdisciplinary Perspectives*, ed. Susan R. Fussell (Mahwah, N.J.: L. Erlbaum Associates, 2002), 79-80.

[21] Authors' pun on *man* (singular for the subject of this chapter) and the *manoeuvres* or *strategies* men employ.

[22] Glen O. Gabbard, *Psychodynamic Psychiatry in Clinical Practice* (Washington: American Psychiatric Publishing, 2005).

[23] Christopher Bollas, *Hysteria* (London: Routledge, 2000); Mardi J. Horowitz, *Hysterical Personality* (NJ: Jason Aronson, 1977).

[24] Mardi J. Horowitz, 'Histrionic Personality Disorder,' in *Treatments of Psychiatric Disorders*, ed. Glen O. Gabbard (Washington: American Psychiatric Publishing, 2001), 2293-2307.

[25] See Shapiro, *Neurotic Styles*; Gabbard, *Psychodynamic Psychiatry*.

[26] Michael H. Stone, 'Schizoid and Schizotypal Personality Disorders,' in *Treatments of Psychiatric Disorders*, ed. Glen O. Gabbard (Washington: American Psychiatric Publishing, 2005), 2237-2250.

[27] See Shapiro, *Neurotic styles*.

[28] Reid J. Meloy, *The Psychopathic Mind: Origins, Dynamics and Treatment* (NJ: Jason Aronsons, 1988).
[29] Glen O. Gabbard, Judith S. Beck and Jeremy Holmes, eds., *Oxford Textbook of Psychotherapy* (Oxford: Oxford University Press, 2005).
[30] Michael Bamberg, 'Language, Concepts and Emotions: The Role of Language in the Construction of Emotions,' *Language Sciences* 19:4 (1997): 309.
[31] Ibid., 310.
[32] Galasiński, *Men and Language,* 73.
[33] Ibid., 73.
[34] See Galasiński, *Man and Language*, 73-75.
[35] Andrzej Leszczyński, 'Woman as Other,' in *Owoc tamtego grzechu* [*The Fruit of That Sin*] (Gdańsk: Wydawnictwo Myślnik, 2013), 182-201.
[36] Galasiński, *Men and Language,* 52.
[37] Ibid., 65.
[38] Dariusz Galasiński, *Language of Deception* (London: Sage Publications, 1998).
[39] By Suzanne Collins (2008-2010).
[40] By Veronica Roth (2011-2013).
[41] *The Big Bang Theory*, Chuck Lorre and Bill Prady (writers and producers), Distributed by Warner Bros. Television, 2007-.
[42] Galasiński, *Men and Language*, 37.
[43] Ibid., 27.
[44] Ibid.
[45] Ibid.
[46] Roger Horrocks, *Masculinity in Crisis: Myths, Fantasies and Realities* (NY: St. Martin, 1994), 30.
[47] Victor J. Seidler, *Unreasonalble Men* (London: Routlegde, 1994), 30.
[48] Krzysztof Hejwowski, 'Communicative Scepticism and the Iissue of Translatability,' *Studia Germanica Gedanensia* 14 (2006): 56.

Bibliography

Bamberg, Michael. 'Language, Concepts and Emotions: The Role of Language in the Construction of Emotions.' *Language Sciences* 19:4 (1997): 309-340.

Bauman, Zygmunt. *Liquid Fear.* Cambridge: Polity Press, 2008.

Bollas, Christopher. *Hysteria.* London: Routledge, 2000.

Fiehler, Reinhard. 'How to Do Emotions with Words: Emotionality in Conversations.' In *The Verbal Communication of Emotions: Interdisciplinary Perspectives*, edited by Susan R. Fussell, 79-106. Mahwah, N.J.: L. Erlbaum Associates, 2002.

Furedi, Frank. *Culture of Fear Revisited. Risk-Taking and the Morality of Low Expectation.* London: Continuum, 2009.

Gabbard, Glen O. *Psychodynamic Psychiatry in Clinical Practice.* Washington: American Psychiatric Publishing, 2005.

Gabbard, Glen, Judith S. Beck, and Jeremy Holmes, eds. *Oxford Textbook of Psychotherapy.* Oxford: Oxford University Press, 2005.

Galasiński, Dariusz. *Men and the Language of Emotions.* New York: Palgrave Macmilan, 2004.

Galasiński, Dariusz. *Language of Deception.* London: Sage Publications, 1998.

Glassner, Barry. *The Culture of Fear: Why Americans Are Afraid of the Wrong Things.* New York: Basic Books, 1999.

Hejwowski, Krzysztof. 'Communicative Scepticism and the Issue of Translatability.' *Studia Germanica Gedanensia* 14 (2006): 49-56.

Horowitz, Mardi J. 'Histrionic Personality Disorder.' In *Treatments of Psychiatric Disorders*, edited by Glen O. Gabbard, 2293-2307. Washington: American Psychiatric Publishing, 2001.

Horrocks, Roger *Masculinity in Crisis: Myths, Fantasies and Realities.* NY: St. Martin, 1994.

Kernberg, Otto F. 'Pathological Narcissism and Narcissistic Personality Disorder: Theoretical Background and Diagnostic Classification.' In *Disorders of Narcissism: Diagnostic, Clinical and Empirical Implications*, edited by Elsa F. Ronningstam, 29-51. Washington: American Psychiatric Press, 1998.

Kohut, Heinz. *The Analysis of the Self: A Systematic Approach to the Psychoanalytic Treatment of Narcissistic Personality Disorders.* NY: International Universities Press, 1971.

Kövecses, Zoltán. *Metaphor and Emotion. Language, Culture, and Body in Human Feeling*. Cambridge: Cambridge University Press, 2007.

Lakoff, George and Mark Johnson. *Metaphors We Live By*. Chicago, London: The University of Chicago Press, 2003.

Leszczyński, Andrzej. *Owoc tamtego grzechu* [*The Fruit of That Sin*], Gdańsk: Wydawnictwo Myślink, 2013.

Lupton, Deborah. *Emotional Self: A Sociocultural Exploration*. London: Sage Publications, 1998.

Seidler, Victor J. *Unreasonalble Men*. London: Routlegde, 1994.

Shapiro, David. *Neurotic Styles*. NY: Basic Books, 1965.

Svendsen, Lars. *Philosophy of Fear*. London: Reaktion Books, 2008.

Wierzbicka, Anna. *Emotions across Languages and Cultures*. Cambridge: Cambridge University Press, 1999.

Žižek, Slavoj. *Demanding the Impossible*. Cambridge: Polity Press, 2013.

Izabela Dixon, PhD, specialises in cognitive linguistics, metaphor and the study of contemporary fears and anxieties. She has published numerous articles on a wide range of subjects including conceptual metaphors of fear and evil, cognitive definitions of monsters, ethno-linguistics, US and THEM schema and aspects of the 'war on terror' discourse.

Magdalena Hodalska, PhD, was a freelance reporter and is now a Senior Lecturer in the Institute of Journalism, Media and Social Communication at the Jagiellonian University in Kraków, Poland. Her research interests are media narratives, discourse and language, war correspondence and fear in the media.

Anxiety in Children with Dyslexia: A Cross-Cultural Study between Indonesia and Germany

Shally Novita and Evelin Witruk

Abstract

The role of emotions in students' reading and writing performance has been shown to result in a heightened levels of anxiety in individuals with dyslexia.[1] However, the type of anxiety generated by dyslexia remains unclear. Although numerous studies found the significance of culture in the shaping of anxiety profile of its members,[2] most studies in this area have so far been conducted mostly in the individualistic cultures. This study investigates the relationship between dyslexia and anxiety, as well as cultural differences in forming particular anxiety types. A total of 163 children from Indonesia and Germany participated in this study. The children were either with or without dyslexia. They completed the Spence Children's Anxiety Scale (SCAS) questionnaire which was based on the *DSM-IV*.[3] A Partial Least Squares Model (PLS) and Multivariate Analysis of Variance (MANOVA) were used to analyse the hypotheses. The obtained results show that children with dyslexia exhibit higher generalized anxiety and separation anxiety from their parents than their peers not suffering from dyslexia. It has also been found that Indonesian children are more anxious of the separation from parents than German children, who are more prone to social phobias.

Key Words: Dyslexia, anxiety, cross-cultural study.

*****

1. Introduction

Historical records indicate that oral communication dominated human cultures for many centuries and such skills as reading and writing, not being natural, had to be developed. With time, written systems superseded or, at least, supplemented the oral tradition as written language was deemed more practical for storing and disseminating information.

For centuries, the skills of reading and writing were denied to most people, it is hardly surprising then that making them available came with a price. Nowadays, reading and writing are considered to be among the most essential and practical requirements of the modern world. The importance attached to the acquisition of these skills sometimes causes a lot of stress, particularly to individuals who have difficulties in dealing with reading and writing acquisition (i.e., dyslexia). Individuals with dyslexia have to deal with both the primary symptoms (i.e., difficulties in reading and writing) and the secondary symptoms (e.g., self-esteem and anxiety issues) as further consequences of their difficulties.

Dyslexia is a specific learning difficulty (LD) that has a neurobiological origin.[4] Being a type of LD, dyslexia has a strong connection to, and thus cannot be separated from other forms of LD. Dyslexia is characterized by difficulties with accurate and/or fluent word recognition as well as by poor spelling and decoding abilities.[5] These difficulties typically result from a deficit in the phonological component of language that is often unexpected in relation to other cognitive abilities and the provision of effective classroom instruction.[6] According to the Diagnostic and Statistical Manual 5 (*DSM-5*),[7] the LD (including dyslexia) are not better accounted for by intellectual disabilities, uncorrected visual or auditory acuity, other mental or neurological disorders, psychosocial adversity, lack of proficiency in the language of academic instruction, or inadequate educational instruction.

Higher level of anxiety in children with LD, particularly children with dyslexia, is the evidence of the role of emotion in academic and reading-writing performance. A number of independent scientific studies pointed to the co-morbidity of dyslexia or secondary symptoms of dyslexia,[8] which was also supported by several meta-analyses.[9] Specifically, children between the ages of 8 and 12 with mild reading disabilities had lower positive well-being scores and were less happy and more anxious than their normal reading peers.[10] Similar anxiety problems were also reported by university students who were diagnosed with dyslexia.[11] This indicates that anxiety issues of individuals with dyslexia could become permanent in adulthood.

Rather contradictory results regarding the relationship between anxiety and dyslexia are also in circulation. Lamm and Epstein conducted a study in order to evaluate emotional status of students with a specific learning difficulty in comparison with student without a given learning difficulty.[12] Specifically, they compared the Hopkins Symptom Checklist (HSCL-90) profiles of 133 adolescent and young adults (38 subjects with developmental dyslexia, 28 subjects with subjective complaints regarding general concentration and reading comprehension difficulties, 23 psychiatric patients, and 44 skilled readers without any known emotional difficulties). A cluster analysis of those subjects did not find any significant differences between the subjects with dyslexia and the control group. Both groups, on the other hand, were easily differentiated from psychiatric patients. Similar results were reported by a study conducted by Miller, Hynd, and Miller.[13] They asked the school-age children with reading problems to rate their own internalizing symptoms. Moreover, the parents and teachers were also asked to do a similar task. As a result, three different reports (i.e., from the children, from the parents and from the teachers) were obtained. The results of this study showed that the children with dyslexia did not develop higher anxiety, depression, and somatization. Additionally, the children who had the lowest score of reading test reported to have similar internalizing symptoms with children who had less reading difficulty.

There are three major reasons for the somewhat contradicting results with regard to the relationship between anxiety and dyslexia. First of all, the cited studies do not provide conclusive evidence as concerns the relationship between self-esteem and dyslexia. As regards the relationship between anxiety and dyslexia, it should be stressed that it is very complex as it involves many factors such as type of anxiety, personality, and environmental issues, all of which may be of significance. Because the relationship is quite dynamic it should be analysed by very sophisticated tools and methods.

Secondly, both the tools for diagnosing dyslexia as well as treatments keep evolving hence the use of even a slightly different approach to the study of dyslexia is likely to produce different results. This situation is hardly surprising because the perception of dyslexia has changed considerably between 1989 and 2013. Therefore, it would not be much of an exaggeration to say that the rather unstable theoretical basis and the changing methods have contributed to some enrichment, if not some confusion.

Thirdly, the continuously evolving theoretical basis for the study of dyslexia opens up new perspectives, which give rise to new paradigms. Despite the fact that these developments may be in some ways limiting, as some questions may remain unanswered, the new studies investigate the relationship between anxiety and dyslexia in the ways dyslexia has not been tested before. Novel approaches take into account contexts and variables, which had previously been neglected, thus producing sometimes challenging results.

The relationship between anxiety and academic achievement is specific to children with dyslexia.[14] Several studies have reported that children and teenagers with dyslexia suffer as a result of their reading and writing deficits and that they have lower levels of perceived scholastic competence,[15] achievement, effort investment, academic efficacy, sense of coherence, positive mood and hope.[16] Over time, children who show high levels of anxiety may experience negative educational outcomes, such as failure to complete high school or college.[17]

However, the processing efficiency theory proposed a possibly contradictory result.[18] The theory assumes that the main effects of worry are on the central executive of the working memory. According to this theory, since worry always impairs performance of tasks which require short-term memory, two major consequences should be expected. First, the storage and processing capacity of the working memory system available for a concurrent task will be reduced even further. As a consequence, any adverse effects of anxiety on performance tend to be greater when tasks impose substantial demands on the capacity of the working memory system, especially if those demands are primarily on the central executive and the articulatory loop. Second, there is an increment in on-task effort and activities designed to improve performance. It is argued that anxious individuals try to cope with threat and worry by allocating additional resources (i.e., effort) and or initiating processing activities (i.e., strategies). It brings two major advantages:

first, they have the chance to block the worrisome thoughts and second, they are able to avoid the more likely poor academic performance. Such attempts, if successful, increase available working memory capacity. Following these two assumptions, it may be stressed that the essential differentiation between the quality of performance (performance effectiveness) and the ratio between performance effectiveness and effort (processing efficiency) should be taken into consideration. Finally, it may be stated that anxiety has more significant effect on efficiency than effectiveness.

Furthermore, the significant role of culture in shaping the anxiety profile of its members has been indicated by a number of scientific cross-cultural studies.[19] Hofstede introduced the Uncertainty Avoidance Index (UAI) dimension as an important factor in the studies of cultural differences.[20] This dimension demonstrates how a particular culture manages ambiguous situations and how strongly culture is related to anxiety.[21] If people tend to have high UAI, it is more likely that they will become anxious toward uncertainty. Accordingly, Indonesia has score of 48 and Germany has score of 65 for UAI and therefore, theoretically, German people are more likely to have higher anxiety in comparison to Indonesian people.

More specifically, in an attempt to comprehend the cultural impact on psychopathological conditions, Kraeplin observed the manifestations and incidences of depression in Java, Indonesia. In his earlier, but still influential article, he anticipated major tasks and issues of cross-cultural or comparative study of psychopathology:

> If the characteristics of a people are manifested in its religion and its customs, in its intellectual artistic achievements, in its political acts and its historical development, then they will also find expression in the frequency and clinical formation of its mental disorders, especially those that emerge from internal conditions. Just as the knowledge of morbid psychic phenomena has opened up for us deep insights into the working of our psychic life, so we may also hope that the psychiatric characteristics of a people can further our understanding of its entire psychic character. In this sense, comparative psychiatry may be destined to one day become an important auxiliary science to comparative ethno-psychology.[22]

Accordingly, Draguns and Tanaka-Matsumi noted that the scope of variation of psychopathological manifestations across cultures are considerable. They also suggested that future investigations should involve generic relationship between psychological disturbances and culture and the specific links between cultural characteristics and psychopathology.[23]

There is a feature that mediates the relationship between culture and social anxiety: the *social behavioural norm*.[24] With regard to this factor, two competing hypotheses have been recognized. It is assumed that countries with clear, strict social norms (e.g., most Asian, African, Southern European and South American countries) are characterised by lower levels of social anxiety than countries in which social behaviour is less norm-governed (e.g., Western European and North American countries).[25] In countries with clear social norms, individuals know precisely what is expected of them, which may reduce social distress. However, because the consequences of breaking social norms in countries with clear and extensive social rules are greater than in countries with more relaxed social rules, the opposite hypothesis may also be true.

It has been found that African-American children experience greater separation anxiety than European-American children.[26] However, their social anxiety is significantly lower than that found in European-American children. This result is consistent with a study conducted by Lewis-Fernandez,[27] who found that the prevalence of social anxiety disorders in the United States is higher than that was found in South Korea, China, Japan, South Africa, Australia, Nigeria and Mexico. These findings indicate that cultural features have considerable impacts on shaping the anxiety profiles and therefore should be considered as an important variable on the anxiety research.

Based on the studies above, the following hypotheses may be constructed. Firstly, children with dyslexia have higher anxiety than children without dyslexia (hypothesis 1). Furthermore, it may be assumed that Indonesian children have higher separation anxiety (hypothesis 2) but lower social phobia (hypothesis 3) as compared to German children.

2. Sample

A total of 163 children from Indonesia (n = 98, M_{age} = 8.73) and Germany (n = 65, M_{age} = 9.42) participated in this study. The ratio between children with and without dyslexia was 71 (M_{age} = 9.27) to 92 (M_{age} = 8.80). The children were assigned to the second (n = 2), third (n = 70), fourth (n = 85), and fifth (n = 6) grade.

The Indonesian group had following characteristics: 38 children with dyslexia and 60 children without dyslexia; 2 second, 46 third, 44 fourth, and 6 fifth graders; 49 boys and 49 girls. The German group consisted of 33 children with dyslexia and 32 children without dyslexia, coming from third (n = 24) and fourth (n = 41) year of school, and were represented by both genders (boys, n = 38 and girls, n = 27). The children with dyslexia were diagnosed by qualified psychologists in both countries, and all children without dyslexia had no history of learning difficulties. Four schools and one clinic for dyslexia in Indonesia and two schools with special needs classes for dyslexia in Germany participated in this study.

There are some differences between Indonesia and Germany regarding diagnostic procedures. Because in Indonesia there are no standardized national procedures, psychologists working in private sectors conducted the diagnosis of dyslexia.

Since dyslexia is not as such recognized by the state, the intervention procedures in Indonesia are also various, and in most of cases they depend on the financial situation of the family. All Indonesian children who participated in this study obtained therapy from either a specialist clinic or attended special needs classes. Some children obtained both programs, which suggests that all Indonesian children with dyslexia came from middle or upper middle class families. Therefore, the children without dyslexia in Indonesia were selected from the similar social background. Even though we could not ask about the financial situation of each family (e.g., salary of parents) due to ethical reasons, we chose schools that are most likely be attended by children coming from at least middle class families.

Special needs classes in Indonesia have relatively standardized program, which means that there are some official regulations in this regard. However, schools tend to implement different approaches. Generally, special needs classes provide: small class size (i.e., ten children with two teachers), daily learning program, and visual media materials. Some schools have more specific programmes such as remedial and modification programmes (e.g., additional lesson, implementation of dyslexia fonts, reducing complexity of test questions, etc.). Furthermore, special needs classes also implement various accommodation tasks, for example, when testing, not only a written test will be conducted, but also an oral exam.

In Germany, the diagnostic procedures for dyslexia vary across the states. In Saxony, where the current study was conducted, there are special needs classes for children with dyslexia that are regulated by the state. All German children with dyslexia who participated in this study were assigned to special needs classes and all children without dyslexia were assigned to mainstream classes in the same schools.

There are some procedures that are usually conducted for the assignment of a child to a special needs class. First step is an official report filed in by teachers regarding the child suspected of having dyslexia. Following these reports, the child is invited to participate in a diagnostic procedure for dyslexia. In most cases, this procedure is conducted during the second grade, but it may also take place at the end of each grade. The diagnosis of dyslexia in Saxony is held over several days. The diagnostic tests are conducted by a team that consists of teachers, educational psychologists and language educationalists.

Special needs classes, with the duration of two years, are available only in some schools. Therefore, some children need to either attend a different school, if they choose to take the recommendation from the diagnostic team. A two-year special class is equivalent to the third grade for children with dyslexia. As a consequence, after two years in the special needs class, the children with dyslexia have to attend the fourth grade with classmates who are one year younger and therefore, they spend five instead of four years in elementary school.

3. Method

The Spence Children's Anxiety Scale (SCAS) was developed by Susan H. Spence in 1994 to assess the severity of anxiety symptoms according to the dimensions of anxiety disorder proposed by the *DSM-IV*.[28] The SCAS evaluates six domains of anxiety: generalised anxiety (example item: *I worry about things*), panic/agoraphobia (example item: *I suddenly feel as if I can't breath when there is no reason for this*), social phobia (example item: *I feel scared when I have to take a test*), separation anxiety (example item: *I worry about being away from my parents*), obsessive-compulsive disorder (example item: *I have to keep checking that I have done things right* [like the switch is off, or the door is locked]), and physical injury fears (example item: *I am scared of dogs, and I am scared of being in high places or a lift*).

There are originally 44 items in SCAS, 38 of which reflect specific symptoms of anxiety and six items related to positive situation to reduce negative response bias. The 38 anxiety items are divided into six subscales: separation anxiety (items 5, 8, 11, 14, and 15), social phobia (items 6, 7, 9, 10, and 25), obsessive compulsive (items 13, 17, 23, 29, and 30), panic/agoraphobia (items 12, 19, 24, 26, and 27), physical injury fears (items 2, 16, 21, 22, and 28), and generalized anxiety (items 1, 3, 4, 18, and 20).

Four possible answers (i.e., never, sometimes, often, and always) were available to describe how often each symptom was experienced. The items were selected from an initial pool of 80 items generated to reflect a broad spectrum of anxiety symptoms. SCAS items were selected from a review of existing literature, clinical experience of four clinical psychologists who specialize in anxiety disorders, child anxiety assessment measures, structured clinical interviews, and the *DSM-IV* diagnostic criteria. If items clearly pertained to a specific trauma event or medical condition, they were deleted. The final 38 items were selected following extensive pilot testing.

Because of time limitation for data collection, only 30 items were included in this study. The unused items were: six positive items and eight items from different subscales so that each subscale has exactly similar quantity of items. This modification reduced the time needed to conduct the SCAS.

Internal consistency of SCAS was examined using a total sample of 2052 children (age = 8-12 years old).[29] The analysis produced a co-efficient alpha of .92 and a Guttman split half reliability of .90. The internal consistency of the subscales was also acceptable, with Cronbach's alphas of .82 (panic/agoraphobia), .70 (separation anxiety), .70 (social phobia), .60 (physical injury fears), .73 (obsessive-compulsive), and .73 (generalized anxiety).[30]

For the current study, the SCAS was translated into Indonesian and German and translated back into English by six psychologists (Cronbach's alpha-Indonesia = .80 and Cronbach's alpha-Germany = .89).

Moreover, teachers were asked to rate the children's academic achievement using a five-option scale: very low, low, middle, high and very high. This method was used for three reasons. Firstly, teachers are the individuals who know and directly and/or repeatedly measure and evaluate children's academic performance. Secondly, countries and even schools implement different methods to assess students' academic achievements. Finally, because the main objective of this study was to investigate secondary symptoms of children with dyslexia from different cultures, using too many measurement tools or items to measure school performance was unnecessary and could have reduced teachers' and students' motivation to participate in this study.

The analysis was conducted through Partial Least Squares (PLS), using the *Smart PLS* software programme. This method was chosen because the PLS method is more robust when used with small sample sizes than covariant-based methods such as Structural Equation Model (SEM), and a small sample size is a limitation of this study.[31]

Because PLS has high sensitivity regarding missing value, special concern toward missing values was made in order to ensure the eligibility of data. As regards this, an expectation maximisation (EM) algorithm was applied.

The measurement model was analysed using the reliability and validity results. According to studies in PLS, all reflective endogenous variables in a PLS analysis should yield >.6 for composite reliability, >.7 factor loadings for indicator reliability, and a >.5 Average Variance Extracted (AVE) value. In addition, the loadings for measured variables (MV) and their latent variables (LV) should be higher than the cross-loadings between variables and other latent variables.[32]

Four analyses should be conducted to confirm the fit of the structural model.[33] First, R^2 should be calculated to determine how much of the variance in the endogenous variable is explained by the exogenous variable. Second, a bootstrap procedure should be performed to confirm the significance of the exogenous variable's explanatory power. Third and fourth, effect size (f^2) and prediction relevance (Q^2) should be calculated in order to be able to explain the predictive relevance of the model. Values of f^2 could be calculated from R^2 as follow:

$f^2 = \left(\frac{R^2_{included} - R^2_{excluded}}{1 - R^2_{included}}\right)$, $R^2_{included}$ is the value of R^2 when particular variable treated as endogenous variable, and $R^2_{excluded}$ is R^2 value when variable treated as exogenous variable.

Furthermore, the value of Q^2 is calculated as follows: D is the omission distance, SSE is the sum of squares of prediction errors, and SSO is the sum of squares of observations. The values of SSE and SSO are available after conducting

$$Q^2 = 1 - \left(\frac{\sum_D SSE_D}{\sum_D SSO_D}\right).$$

blindfolding procedure. Q^2 values above zero provide evidence that the observed values are well reconstructed and that the model has predictive relevance, whereas Q^2 values below zero indicate a lack of predictive relevance. Moreover, it might be noted that only in correspondence with f^2, the relative impact of the structural model on the observed measures for latent dependent variables can be assessed: $q^2 = \left(\frac{Q^2_{included} - Q^2_{excluded}}{1 - Q^2_{included}}\right)$. Regarding the importance of calculating f^2, Q^2, and q^2, it is urged that researchers use these statistical criterions to make a stronger case for model predictive capabilities.

4. Results and Discussion

Image 1 is the model developed to explain the relationship between the variables that were stipulated in the hypotheses. PLS results show that the model has composite reliability of more than .6 (.80, .81, and .75 for anxiety, separation anxiety and social phobia respectively). The AVEs for separation anxiety and social phobia are acceptable both being .60. However, the AVE for anxiety is not that high (.46). All cross loadings except panic/agoraphobia have values above .70. Furthermore, because separation anxiety and social phobia are both LVs and MVs for anxiety (second order factor), they have a strong relationship amongst each other.

Table 1: Factor Loadings and Cross Loadings

	Nation	Dyslexia	Achievement	Anxiety	SA	SP
GA	.13	.21	.11	**.54**	.29	.50
PA	-.00	.12	.10	**.52**	.27	.25
PIF	-.32	.10	.08	**.84**	.53	.15
SA	-.27	.14	.05	**.84**	-	.22
OC	-.22	-.12	.00	**.56**	.21	.15
Item 14	-.33	.11	.06	.66	**.82**	.12
Item 8	-.20	.03	.08	.56	**.63**	.04
Item 5	-.31	.11	-.09	.54	**.84**	.03
Item 6	.20	.17	.01	.15	.01	**.85**
Item 9	.15	.03	.02	.22	.15	**.69**

Note. GA = generalized anxiety. PA = panic/agoraphobia. PIF = physical injury fears. SA = separation anxiety. SP = social phobia. Factor loadings between an indicator and its latent variable are in boldface.

Image 1 shows the R^2 of .15, .14, .05, and .00 for anxiety, separation anxiety, social phobia and achievement, respectively. According to these results, the model has a weak-substantial R^2.

Moreover, Table 2 shows that the model has weak-medium effect sizes. According to Image 1, anxiety has a significant effect on separation anxiety and social phobia, dyslexia has a significant effect on anxiety, and country has a significant effect on separation anxiety and social phobia.

Table 2: Effect Sizes and Predictive Relevance

	f^2	Q^2	q^2
Country-separation anxiety	-	.08	-
Country-social phobia	-	.02	-
Country-anxiety	-	.05	-
Dyslexia-anxiety	-.03	.05	.01
Dyslexia-achievement	.00	-.00	-.00
Achievement-anxiety	-.01	.05	.01

Note. Interpretation of the values f^2: .02 = weak, .15 = medium, .33 = large effect.[34] Q^2-values below zero indicate lack of predictive relevance.[35] It was not possible to analyse the f^2 and q^2 of the path nation-separation anxiety, nation-social phobia, and nation-anxiety.

Image 1 delivers information regarding beta values/path coefficients and significant results (paths with a star reflect a significant beta value).

Table 3: Two Ways ANOVA (Country x Dyslexia) for Anxiety

Subscales	$F_{country}$	$F_{dyslexia}$	$F_{interaction}$
Anxiety	4.73*	3.68	.38
Generalized anxiety	1.82	6.05*	.23
Panic/agoraphobia	.01	2.92	1.64
Social phobia	1.84	3.00	.44
Separation anxiety	15.47**	3.90*	2.29
Obsessive compulsive	7.57**	1.33	.00
Physical injury fears	20.36**	2.78	.40

Note. $n_{Indonesia}$ = 98. $n_{Germany}$ = 65. $n_{dyslexia}$ = 71. $n_{nondyslexia}$ = 92. * = $p < .05$. ** = $p < .01$. Code for country: 1 = Germany, 2 = Indonesia. Code for dyslexia: 1 = non-dyslexia, 2 = dyslexia.

Additionally to investigate the interaction effect between the country and dyslexia, a two way MANOVA (country x dyslexia) was calculated for anxiety and its six subtypes (see Table 3). According to these results, Indonesian and German children are different in terms of their anxiety, separation anxiety, physical injury fears, and obsessive-compulsions, whereas children with and without dyslexia are different in terms of their separation and generalized anxieties. No interaction effect was found for this analysis. There are differences between PLS and MANOVA regarding the effect of country on social phobia. PLS reported a significant effect of country on social phobia, while MANOVA did not confirm this result. This difference was probably due to the different calculation processes of both methods.

Based on the results above, the first hypothesis of this study was not confirmed. Dyslexia could bring negative impacts such as anxiety issues,[36] but with some appropriate treatments the secondary symptoms of dyslexia could be avoided. In the current study, most of the children with dyslexia were assigned to special needs classes from which they might have benefited. In the special needs classes, all students have similar difficulties in reading and writing. These circumstances will maintain their self-esteem and yield the feeling of security. Also, in the special needs classes, different standards of academic achievement and curriculum are applied. As a consequence, the teachers have more flexible purposes to achieve and the students do not need to struggle and push themselves to obtain similar reading and writing scores as compared to other students without dyslexia, particularly because this could give them the sense of unfairness.

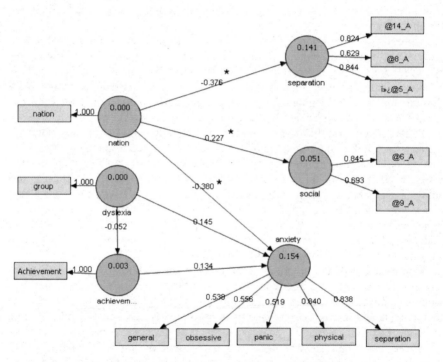

Image 1: Partial Least Squares model for the relationship between dyslexia, anxiety and cultural differences. Numbers inside the circles = R^2. Numbers between circles and rectangles = factor loadings. Numbers between two circles = beta values/path coefficients. * $p < .05$. © 2014. Courtesy of the author.

Because most studies on anxiety and dyslexia were conducted in individualistic western cultures, there is a pressing need to conduct similar studies involving collectivist cultures. The problem is that the studies and results concerning the cases of dyslexia in Germany when applied to children with dyslexia from Indonesia could raise some considerable issues. The primary issue is related to cultural differences between Germany and Indonesia. Since individualistic cultures urge independence in children so that they could be more successful in life, collectivistic cultures emphasize social help and the idea that no one could achieve success without others. Based on this assumption it may be implied that parents of German children with dyslexia may not assist their children as much as Indonesian parents do. As a consequence, Indonesian children with dyslexia are more emotionally independent than German children with a similar difficulty. This may lead to different findings regarding the secondary symptoms of dyslexia between the children from these two countries.

Moreover, some studies do not find any significant differences between individuals with and without dyslexia regarding their internalizing symptoms, however, both groups were clearly different from psychiatric patients.[37] These results indicate that even though there are some indications that individuals with dyslexia may develop high anxiety level, it is too early to conclude that secondary symptoms of dyslexia such as clinical emotional problems will always occur.

Regarding cultural differences and anxiety, Compton and colleagues undertook a study with 2.384 non-clinical and 217 clinical children and adolescents.[38] They found that children in collectivist cultures experience more separation anxiety but lower social anxiety in comparison to children from individualistic cultures. In this study, Indonesian children with dyslexia reported greater separation anxiety, obsessive-compulsion, fears of physical injury and lower social phobia. The incidence of other types of anxiety was similar for the two countries, indicating that the current study supports Compton's findings regarding the role of culture in shaping the social anxiety profile of its members.

Indonesian children in comparison to German children, were found more anxious if separated from their parents and/or if they were left alone. Because they have been raised in a collectivist culture, Indonesian children are more attached to their parents and family than their German counterparts and therefore they become more anxious in the situations that require them to be alone. Moreover, according to Kirmayer, cultures vary in the composition of family, maternal-infant interaction, and child-rearing practice.[39] As an individualistic culture, Germans highly appreciate self-actualization and put the independence of children as one of the primary educational factors.[40] For instance, it is common for German children to go to school by themselves, whereas most of the middle class Indonesian parents prefer to accompany their children as they go to elementary school. While for German children doing daily activities by themselves or being alone at home is a common experience, the same situation would evoke separation anxiety in Indonesian children.

Furthermore, Hofstede established that in Germany attention to detail is essential in order to create certainty. Consequently, each topic or project is very well-thought-out.[41] In line with this characteristic German healthcare system and responses to emergencies are far better than those in Indonesia. A well-developed system provides a feeling of security, which is also supported by high precision and attachment to rules. Unfortunately, the healthcare and emergency systems in Indonesia are not entirely efficient. It is then not surprising that uncertainty, particularly regarding protection of one's physical health are assumed to be the main reason why Indonesian children have higher physical injury fears than German children.

With regard to children with dyslexia, all German children with dyslexia in the current study were assigned to special needs classes run by the state. Educational costs in Germany are mostly financed by the state. All school-age children must obtain appropriate education, which is free of charge, except when parents want their children to have particular curriculum that is not supported by the state schools (e.g., international or reform educational schools). In this case, children need to go to private schools. Moreover, if children cannot show superior academic achievements or have no intention to go to university, they have an option to engage themselves in vocational schools that are run by the state.

To be concluded, Germany with their high UAI has provided their people with higher sense of security because Germany has a very well-established system of social care. On the contrary, Indonesia has a lower score of UAI. Indonesians believe that the future cannot be controlled and that the life is too complex to be fully understood and controlled. According to Hofstede, this flexible approach to reality and could reduce tension and anxiety. However, this flexibility may also cause problems since it offers mainly uncertainty and thus little security. Indonesian social welfare system is not as comprehensive as the German system, for example, Indonesia does not provide a standardized health care system for its citizens. Some medical treatments and interventions are available privately and are therefore inaccessible for families with low incomes.

Indonesian educational system is also less efficient than the German system. In Germany, all schools have comparable standards of facilities and teachers. In Indonesia, some schools are poorly equipped and understaffed, whereas others have outstanding facilities and teaching staff. Moreover, lack of teachers who specialize in dyslexia is also a major problem in Indonesia.

In this day and age, education is very competitive. Because Indonesian schools compare less favourably to schools in Germany, it is not surprising that school enrolment in Indonesia is more competitive. It is therefore not much of overstatement to say that education in Indonesia is more of a business or even a commodity which favours well-situated children or children with high academic potential.

All Indonesian children who took part in the presented study came at least from middle class families. Having this or higher social status, put children in a rather privileged position in terms of educational opportunities. The dyslexic study subjects needed specialist support, which was not provided by the state schools.

Summarising, it may be stated that with insufficient support with regard to such basic skills as reading and writing and/or education in general, anxiety of Indonesian children is likely to be heightened. Germany offers more security to their community members, which reduces the incidence of anxiety. The feeling of safety regarding education is very important to children, who recognize the importance of education for their life prospects. Because of significant differences between Indonesian and German educational systems, particularly regarding support from the state for special needs education and/or education in general, Indonesian children have higher anxiety than German children.

As regards the presented study, following recommendations can be made. Firstly, the sample size was not sufficiently big and therefore should be increased in order to achieve more reliable results. Unfortunately, availability of dyslexic students affects the sample size of most studies on various aspects of dyslexia. Secondly, this study did not differentiate between the treatments obtained by the children with dyslexia. Even though the treatments for dyslexia have similar main purpose (i.e., increasing the reading and writing ability), they may vary in specific purposes (i.e., increasing self-esteem, reducing anxiety, depression, building up positive attitude, etc.). Because the children with dyslexia in this study did not obtain similar treatments, they may also vary in their personal and emotional development.

Notes

[1] Julia M. Caroll and Jane E. Iles, 'An Assessment of Anxiety Level of Dyslexic Students in Higher Education,' *British Journal of Educational Psychology* 76 (2006): 651-62.
[2] Nina Heinrichs, Ronald M. Rapee, Lynn A. Alden, Susan Boegels, Stefan G. Hofmann, Kyung J. Oh and Yuji Sakano, 'Cultural Differences in Perceived Social Norms and Social Anxiety,' *Behaviour Research and Therapy* 44 (2006): 1187-97.
[3] Susan H. Spence, 'A Measure of Anxiety Symptoms among Children,' *Behaviour Research and Therapy* 36 (1998): 545-66.
[4] Reid G. Lyon, Sally E. Shaywitz and Bennett A. Shaywitz, 'Defining Dyslexia, Comorbidity, Teachers' Knowledge of Language and Writings,' *Annals of Dyslexia* 53 (2003): 1-15.
[5] Ibid., 5.

[6] Ibid., 7.

[7] American Psychiatric Association, ed., *Diagnostic and Statistical Manual of Mental Disorders* (Fifth Edition, Arlington, VA: American Psychiatric Publishing, 2013).

[8] Caroll and Iles, 'An Assessment of Anxiety,' 651-62; Norah Frederickson and Sarah Jacobs, 'Controllability Attributions for Academic Performance and the Perceived Scholastic Competence, Global Self-Worth and Achievement of Children with Dyslexia,' *School Psychology International* 22 (2001): 401-16; Timothy D. Lackaye and Malka Margalit, 'Comparison of Achievement, Effort, and Self-Perception among Students with Learning Disabilities and Their Peers from Different Achivement Groups,' *Journal of Learning Disabilities* 39 (2006): 432-46.

[9] Kenneth A. Kavale and Steven R. Forness, 'Social Skill Deficit and Learning Disabilities: A Meta-Analysis,' *Journal of Learning Disabilities* 29 (1996): 226-37; Jason M. Nelson and Hannah Harwood, 'Learning Disabilities and Anxiety: A Meta-Analysis,' *Journal of Learning Disabilities* 44 (2011): 3-17; Thomson H. Prout, Steven D. Marcal and Debra C. Marcal, 'A Meta-Analysis of Self-Reported Personality Characteristics of Children and Adolescents with Learning Abilities,' *Journal of Psychoeducational Assessment* 10 (1992): 59-64.

[10] Rosemary Casey, Susann E Levy, Kimberly Brown and J. Brooks-Gunn, 'Impaired Emotional Health in Children with Mild Reading Disability,' *Developmental and Behavioural Pediatrics* 13 (1992): 256-60.

[11] Caroll and Iles, 'An Assessment of Anxiety,' 651-62.

[12] Oren Lamm and Rachel Epstein, 'Specific Reading Impairment: Are They to be Associated with Emotional Difficulties?,' *Journal of Learning Disabilities* 25 (1992): 605-615.

[13] Carlin J. Miller, George W. Hynd, and Scott R. Miller, 'Children with Dyslexia: Not Necessarily at Risk for Elevated Internalizing Symptoms,' *Reading and Writing* 18 (2005): 425-436.

[14] Casey, Levy, Brown, and Brooks-Gunn, 'Impaired Emotional Health in Children,' 256-60.

[15] Frederickson, and Jacobs, 'Controllability Attributions,' 401.

[16] Lackaye, and Margalit, 'Comparison of Achievement,' 432.

[17] Michael Van Ameringen, Catherine Mancini and Peter Farvolden, 'The Impact of Anxiety Disorders on Educational Achievement,' *Journal of Anxiety Disorders* 17 (2003): 561-71; Ronald C. Kessler, Cindy L. Foster, William B. Saunders, and Paul E. Stang, 'Social Consequences of Psychiatric Disorders, I: Educational Attainment,' *Am J Psychiatry* 152 (1995): 1036-32.

[18] Michael W. Eysenck and Manuel G. Calvo, 'Anxiety and Performance: The Processing Efficiency Theory,' *Cognition and Emotion* 6 (1992): 409-434.

[19] Scott N. Compton, Aimee H. Nelson, and John S. March, 'Social Phobia and Separation Anxiety Symptoms in Community and Clinical Samples of Children and Adolescents,' *Child and Adolescent Psychiatry* 39.8 (2000): 1040-46; Heinrichs, Rapee, Alden, Boegels, Hofmann, Oh and Sakano, 'Cultural Differences,' 1187-97; Stefan G Hofmann, Anu Asnaani and Devon E. Hinton, 'Cultural Aspects in Social Anxiety and Social Anxiety Disorders,' *Depress Anxiety* 27.12 (2010): 1117-27.

[20] Geert Hofstede, *Culture's Consequences: Comparing Values, Behaviors, Institutions, and Organizations across Nations* (Second Edition, Thousand Oaks: Sage Publication, 2001).

[21] Geert Hofstede, *Culture's Consequences*, 2; Geert Hofstede, Geert J. Hofstede and Michael Minkov, *Cultures and Organizations. Software of the Mind* (Revised and Expanded Third Edition, New York: McGraw Hill, 2010).

[22] Emil Kraeplin, 'Vergleichende Psychiatrie' [Comparative Psychiatry], *Zentralblatt duer Nervenheilkunde und Psychiatrie* 27 (1904): 433-437.

[23] Juris G. Draguns and Junko Tanaka-Matsumi, 'Assessment of Psychopathology across and within Cultures: Issues and Findings,' *Behaviour Research and Therapy* 41 (2003): 755-76.

[24] Heinrichs, et al., 'Cultural Differences,' 1188.

[25] Ibid., 1195.

[26] Compton, Nelson, and March, 'Social Phobia,' 1040.

[27] Roberto Lewis-Fernandez, Devon E. Hinton, Amaro J. Laria, Elissa H. Patterson, Stefan G. Hofmann, Michelle G. Craske, Dan J. Stein, Anu Asnaani and Betty Liao, 'Culture and the Anxiety Disorders: Recommendations for DSM-V,' *Depression and Anxiety* 0 (2009): 1-18.

[28] Spence, 'A Measure of Anxiety,' 545-66.

[29] Spence, 'A Measure of Anxiety,' 558.

[30] Ibid.

[31] James Gaskin, 'Pls, Gaskination'S Statwiki,' 11 July 2013, viewed on 12 February 2014. http://statwiki.kolobkreations.com; Nils Urbach and Frederik Ahlemann, 'Structural Equation Modelling in Information Systems Research Using Partial Least Squares,' *Journal of Information Technology Theory and Application* 11.2 (2010): 5-40.

[32] Joerg Hanseler, Christian M. Ringle and Rudolf R. Sinkovics, 'The Use of Partial Least Squares Path Modeling in International Marketing,' *Advances in International Marketing* 20 (2009): 277-319.

[33] Ibid., 298-310.

[34] Jacob Cohen, *Statistical Power Analysis for the Behavioural Science* (Second Edition, Hilsdale, NJ: Lawrence Erlbaum Associates Publishers, 1988).

[35] Hanseler, Ringle and Sinkovics, 'The Use of Partial,' 303.

[36] Caroll and Iles, 'An Assessment of Anxiety,' 651.
[37] Lamm and Epstein, 'Specific Reading Impairment,' 605.
[38] Compton, Nelson and March, 'Social Phobia,' 1040.
[39] Laurence J Kirmayer, 'Cultural Variations in the Clinical Presentation of Depression and Anxiety: Implications for Diagnosis and Treatment,' *Journal of Clinical Psychiatry* 62.13 (2001): 22-28.
[40] Hofstede, Hofstede, and Minkov, *Cultures and Organizations*, 117-118.
[41] Ibid., 188-224.

Bibliography

American Psychiatric Association, ed. *Diagnostic and Statistical Manual of Mental Disorders.* Fifth Edition, Airlington, VA: American Psychiatric Publishing, 2013.

Caroll, Julia M., and Jane E. Iles. 'An Assessment of Anxiety Level of Dyslexic Students in Higher Education.' *British Journal of Educational Psychology* 76 (2006): 651-62.

Casey, Rosemary, Susann E. Levy, Kimberly Brown and J Brooks-Gunn. 'Impaired Emotional Health in Children with Mild Reading Disability.' *Developmental and Behavioural Pediatrics* 13 (1992): 256-60.

Cohen, Jacob. *Statistical Power Analysis for the Behavioural Science.* Second Edition, Hilsdale, NJ: Lawrence Erlbaum Associates Publishers, 1988.

Compton, Scott N., Aimee H. Nelson, and John S. March. 'Social Phobia and Separation Anxiety Symptoms in Community and Clinical Samples of Children and Adolescents.' *Child and Adolescent Psychiatry* 39.8 (2000): 1040-46.

Draguns, Juris G., and Junko Tanaka-Matsumi. 'Assessment of Psychopathology across and within Cultures: Issues and Findings.' *Behaviour Research and Therapy* 41 (2003): 755-76.

Eysenck, Michael. W. and Manuel G. Calvo. 'Anxiety and Performance: The Processing Efficiency Theory.' *Cognition and Emotion* 6 (1992): 409-434.

Frederickson, Norah, and Sarah Jacobs. 'Controllability Attributions for Academic Performance and the Perceived Scholastic Competence, Global Self-Worth and Achievement of Children with Dyslexia.' *School Psychology International* 22 (2001): 401-16.

Gaskin, James. 'Pls, Gaskination`S Statwiki,' 11 July 2013. Viewed on 12 February 2014. http://statwiki.kolobkreations.com.

Green, Donna H., and Adrian B. Ryans. 'Entry Strategies and Market Performance Causal Modeling of a Business Simulation.' *Journal of Product Innovation Management* 7.1 (1990): 45-58.

Hanseler, Joerg, Christian M. Ringle, and Rudolf R. Sinkovics. 'The Use of Partial Least Squares Path Modeling in International Marketing.' *Advances in International Marketing* 20 (2009): 277-319.

Heinrichs, Nina, Ronald M. Rapee, Lynn A. Alden, Susan Boegels, Stefan G. Hofmann, Kyung J. Oh, and Yuji Sakano. 'Cultural Differences in Perceived Social Norms and Social Anxiety.' *Behaviour Research and Therapy* 44 (2006): 1187-97.

Hofmann, Stefan G., Anu Asnaani, and Devon E Hinton. 'Cultural Aspects in Social Anxiety and Social Anxiety Disorders.' *Depress Anxiety* 27, no. 12 (2010): 1117-27.

Hofstede, Geert. *Culture`s Consequences: Comparing Values, Behaviors, Institutions, and Organizations across Nations.* Second Edition, Thousand Oaks: Sage Publication, 2001.

Hofstede, Geert, Geert J. Hofstede, and Michael Minkov. *Cultures and Organizations. Software of the Mind.* Revised and Expanded 3rd Edition ed. New York: McGraw Hill, 2010.

Kavale, Kenneth A., and Steven R Forness. 'Social Skill Deficit and Learning Disabilities: A Meta Analysis.' *Journal of Learning Disabilities* 29 (1996): 226-37.

Kessler, Ronald C., Cindy L. Foster, William B. Saunders, and Paul E. Stang. 'Social Consequences of Psychiatric Disorders, I: Educational Attainment.' *Am J Psychiatry* 152 (1995): 1036-32.

Kirmayer, Laurence J. 'Cultural Variations in the Clinical Presentation of Depression and Anxiety: Implications for Diagnosis and Treatment.' *Journal of Clinical Psychiatry* 62.13 (2001): 22-28.

Kraeplin, Emil. 'Vergleichende Psychiatrie' [Comparative Psychiatry]. *Zentralblatt duer Nervenheilkunde und Psychiatrie* 27 (1904): 433-437.

Lackaye, Timothy D., and Malka Margalit. 'Comparison of Achievement, Effort, and Self-Perception among Students with Learning Disabilities and Their Peers from Different Achivment Groups.' *Journal of Learning Disabilities* 39 (2006): 432-46.

Lamm, Oren and Rachel Epstein. 'Specific Reading Impairment: Are They to be Associated with Emotional Difficulties?' *Journal of Learning Disabilities* 25 (1992): 605-615.

Lee, Don Y., and Eric W. K. Tsang. 'The Effects of Entrepreneurial Personality, Background and Network Activities on Venture Growth.' *Journal of Management Studies* 38.4 (2001): 583-602.

Lewis-Fernandez, Roberto, Devon E. Hinton, Amaro J. Laria, Elissa H. Patterson, Stefan G. Hofmann, Michelle G. Craske, Dan J. Stein, Anu Asnaani, and Betty Liao. 'Culture and the Anxiety Disorders: Recommendations for DSM-V.' *Depression and Anxiety* 0 (2009): 1-18.

Lyon, Reid G., Sally E. Shaywitz, and Bennett A. Shaywitz. 'Defining Dyslexia, Comorbidity, Teachers' Knowledge of Language and Writings.' *Annals of Dyslexia* 53 (2003): 1-15.

Miller, Carlin J., George W. Hynd, and Scott R. Miller. 'Children with Dyslexia: Not Necessarily at Risk for Elevated Internalizing Symptoms.' *Reading and Writing* 18 (2005): 425-436.

Nelson, Jason M., and Hannah Harwood. 'Learning Disabilities and Anxiety: A Meta Analysis.' *Journal of Learning Disabilities* 44 (2011): 3-17.

Prout, Thomson H., Steven D. Marcal, and Debra C. Marcal. 'A Meta-Analysis of Self-Reported Personality Characteristics of Children and Adolescents with Learning Abilities.' *Journal of Psychoeducational Assessment* 10 (1992): 59-64.

Singelis, Theodore M., and William F. Sharkey. 'Culture, Self-Construal and Embarassability.' *Journal of Cross-Cultural Psychology* 26 (1995): 622-44.

Spence, Susan H. 'A Measure of Anxiety Symptoms among Children.' *Behaviour Research and Therapy* 36 (1998): 545-66.

Urbach, Nils, and Frederik Ahlemann. 'Structural Equation Modeling in Information Systems Research Using Partial Least Squares.' *Journal of Information Technology Theory and Application* 11.2 (2010): 5-40.

Van Ameringen, Michael, Catherine Mancini, and Peter Farvolden. 'The Impact of Anxiety Disorders on Educational Achievement.' *Journal of Anxiety Disorders* 17 (2003): 561-71.

Vigilante, Florence Wexler, and Elizabeth Dane. 'Teenage Dyslexia: Sturm Und Drang.' *Child and Adolescent Social Work* 8.6 (1991): 515-23.

Shally Novita is PhD student at the Leipzig University, Germany.

Evelin Witruk is Professor at the Department of Educational and Rehabilitative Psychology, University of Leipzig, Germany.

Scientific Explanations of Fear and Anxiety Relating to the Choice of Deity

Sukran Karatas

Abstract
Estrangement is one of the biggest causes of fear and anxiety in the twenty-first century to such a degree that individuals are failing to understand and identify the true self even in the big picture, let alone within the complexity of psychology. East and West, physics and metaphysics, body and spirit, you and I and many more things are not only dragged apart from each other, but also divided in its own nature. Non-sentient beings, including the human body, act upon built-in knowledge designed by the same super power behind the Big Bang to perform their finely tuned individual and collective actions completely free from oppression of one another. Human voluntary actions, on the contrary, are initiated by conscious knowledge, become apparent by actions that cooperated with built-in structure. Brain, mind and heart, in particular, are the places that the combined energy waves are generated, received and reflected depending on the values of individual perceptions and genetic abilities. Hence, accurate codes and coordinations are absolutely necessary for emotion-related unsteady voluntary actions to work in harmony with the automated ones. Individuals are free to choose their own deity but it is essential to have the same Deity to establish perfect consistency between the two systems and the Deity. Only then total freedom, equality and justice can be achieved voluntarily in line with the nature. Therefore, my chapter aims to draw attention to existent missing links between the innate and voluntary actions and offering scientific solutions. Arguing that the methods of the existing four types of 'energy wave end boundary behaviours' between the different mediums can be used to assess the authenticity of the relationships between the chooser and the chosen deity, which is vital for human health, wealth, happiness and social relations.

Key Words: Deity, anxiety, peace, energy, power, freedom, equality, justice, psychology, biology, happiness, sadness, hope, fear.

*****

Human beings are the only creations who need to learn how to control their own emotions and arrange individual and social life orders consciously. Their existence involves every aspect of life based on certain kinds of energy networks, seen or unseen. The entire existence, including human body and soul, is closely interwoven with finely tuned codes and coordinations, pre-programmed to work together in perfect harmony. Therefore, it is necessary for humans to know all these already existing authentic structures to establish valid links with them consciously.

Predetermined beings are working from a base of total freedom, equality and justice, which are the vital key factors for harmonious interrelations and a slightest disturbance in any one of these will lead to fundamental chaos in the whole existence. It is the same for consciously chosen human individual and social life orders. Any disturbance in the balance of freedom, equality and justice will be the first main source for fear and anxiety, which can lead to even bigger chaos in the big picture but especially in individual human health, happiness and social relations. Therefore, authentication is the vital basis in obtaining knowledge and choosing a deity to establish valid interrelations within the whole existence including human body, soul and spirit to be able to live a happy and healthy life in peace.

Depending on the scientific developments of time, authentic knowledge can be verified though practical experiments in one way or the other. However, justification of human individual or collective rationale remains as the most problematic issue as ever, even in the twenty-first century. In fact, uncertainties in human reasoning continue to be one of the main causes of fear and anxiety when it comes to identifying the boundaries of the basic life principles, even for self, let alone for others. Basic individual, mutual and universal values are necessary to set the foundation for life order but who is to decide what is right for whom. According to the predetermined systems the existing human beings are all equal, therefore, any human interference will naturally disturb the existing freedom, equality and justice not only within the self, but also among others. Therefore, humans, consciously or unconsciously, turn to choose a deity or deities mostly among supernatural beings. Now, it is high time for human beings to choose their own deity on the basis of scientific authentication without disturbing the three key factors, which are vital for health and happiness.

To be able to understand this quite new and complicated subject well, we have to know the structure and the working system of the universe and the autonomous energy interaction behaviours between the 'Source Power' and the creations, as well as between the creations. We also have to know the history of human beings in relation to choosing a deity or deities and their immediate, retrospective and prospective effects on individuals, cultures and societies. Then, we will

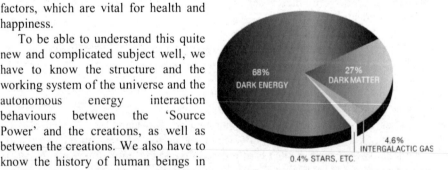

Image 1: Percentages of the Universe
© 2014, Shukran Publishing.
Used with permission.

look into energy wave end behaviours on meeting with different mediums to demonstrate scientific justification for how to choose the authentic deity.

Physical and metaphysical worlds are powered, supported and run by an Invisible Source behind the Big Bang. The Universe contains 68% of Dark Energy, 27% of Dark Matter, 4.5% of Intergalactic gas and 0.4% of Stars, which "... undergo an explosive period of rapid change, in which helium is transformed into carbon, nitrogen, oxygen, silicon, phosphorus, and all the other elements that play vital role in bio-chemistry."[1] Existence in this dimension is acting in harmony due to a pre-programmed system, which bonds each entity within itself, with its surroundings and with its own source, the cosmological constant,[2] and to the power of the highest intellect, the Deity. Actions in this system take place in relation to time and space, in an interval of generating and degenerating spans. The level of these interrelations depends on the number of atoms in the substances and the gravity ratio between them.[3] It has such a perfect energy network in which even the slightest disturbance is not tolerated.

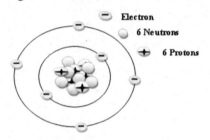

Image 2: Basic Units of Matter.
© 2014, Shukran Publishing.
Used with permission.

Before the nineteenth century atoms were accepted as the basic units of matter but their structure was unknown. At the beginning of the twentieth century, Ernest Rutherford (1871-1937) who was working on atomic radioactivity found out that almost all the particles pass through the gold sheet with little or no deflection...however, an occasional particle bounced back. It must have struck something very dense indeed... Most of the radioactive particles pass freely through the nearly empty space that makes up most of the atom, but a few particles happen to strike the dense mass at the centre and rebound.[4]

In his model, negatively charged orbiting electrons had mass. The positively charged dense nucleus at the centre was made up of two types of particles - protons and neutrons - and the number of protons determined what element that atom is. In addition, the electrons orbiting with the speed of light make the nuclei appear to be surrounded by clouds.[5] Now, we know that matter is composed of atoms that have two numbers. One of them is called the 'atomic number,' which defines the charge of the nucleus, and the other is called the 'atomic weight,' which defines the mass that

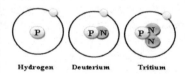

Image 3: Atomic Numbering.
© 2014, Shukran Publishing.
Used with permission.

determines the behaviour of the electrons.[6]

Generally, numbers of orbiting electrons are equal to the numbers of protons in the nucleus, which neutralises the atom 'when an atom contains different number of electrons than protons, the atom is called an Ion. The process of creating an ion is called ionization.'[7] However, the number of neutrons may vary even in the same elements, which are called 'isotopes,' enabling transformation from one element to another. Each radioactive isotope has its own disintegrating (decaying) time to transform from one stage to the other, which is called 'half-life.' Niels Bohr (1885-1962) demonstrated that, when an electron jumps from one energy level to another level 'spectral lines' occur; this discovery is now used to estimate the age of elements.[8] This is another universal law that leads to another leap in science to Quantum Mechanics.

Spectral lines are used to estimate the beginning of existence and the age of matters. Big Bang is said to have taken place approximately 13.7 billion years ago. This was also the beginning of time and space in the dimension that we live in today. However, the entity of the first 10^{-43} second, 'the inflationary epoch' of the Big Bang was infinitely dense atom-size at the beginning but it had the biggest increase in size from atom to orange size at the time of 10^{-32} second. The heat reaction could not be measured owing to its intensity, even with the most advanced technology. At first, the four forces of nature, strong and weak nuclear force, force of gravity and electromagnetic force were not separated. They were combined as one unit that is known as 'singularity.' At the time of 10^{-6} the cooling started to take place, quarks begin to clump into segments and the nuclear gas cloud began to appear. By the time of 3 minutes, the universe seemed to be a clump of fog, which was the time for radiation to begin turning into matter.[9]

Even though gravity and light worked hand-in-hand from the beginning, before the formation of matter, light was not visible. About 300.000 years after the Big Bang matter started to form and the light began to hit it and reflect back. Therefore, light needs matter to be visible; matter needs light to be visible. Surely, waves need matter to hit and reflect back in the dimension of the universe that we live in. The length of the light waves between the source and the matter depend on the density, distance, temperature, characteristics and the shapes of the matter.[10] Waves have their own universal laws, as does gravity. The human physical body is matter. Therefore, it is included in the automatically ruled and regulated category of the like, obeying the laws of gravity and light separately, as well as the combined laws that work together.

On the other hand, spirit has an undetermined free will system alongside the determined form that can be controlled by human free will consciously, able to receive incoming energy waves, evaluate them and send them out towards the intended targets. However, authentic codes and coordinations are necessary to have valid connections and correlations to be able to receive correct amounts of energy from the source and the others, and reflect them back correctly. Thus, the existence of free will can facilitate or impede human beings in choosing, motivating and controlling these energy levels between the self and others, including the Creator. The point of free will is closely related to the choice of deity, the unification of body, soul and spirit, the interrelation with others, human or non-human. There are energy wave connections between the Creator and the creations as well as among the creations. This is another universal law that includes gravity and light waves, which establishes the necessary interconnection to hold all existence together as one unit.

A wave is a travelling disturbance going through a medium. It experiences local oscillations and a regular periodic value that gives information about the character of the medium. This periodic value changes while the disturbance is passing through from one medium to another. We have to remember that particles in the medium stay constant in their places whilst energy in the waves moves

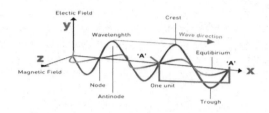

Image 4: A Diagram two waves travelling on the same medium.
© 2014, Shukran Publishing.
Used with permission.

along. There are low and high-energy waves with the ability to carry the energy from one medium to another depending on their strength and they can also travel in opposite directions, collide with each other, and can be absorbed or reflected back depending on the character and the position of the boundary or the barriers that they come across.

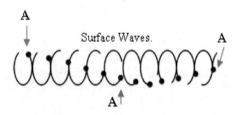

Image 5: Wave movements.
© 2014, Shukran Publishing.
Used with permission.

We have to remind ourselves here that we are talking about only one line of a wave that travels along a particular stream line and demonstrates different behaviour when it reaches its own boundary where it meets a different medium from its own. One unit of a wave is marked when point 'A' in a model circle comes to the same place where it started, then the second unit starts from point 'A' again and so on. The harmonic waves have 'nodes' at the point of each 'A.' Each turn creates a loop and the half-waypoint is called 'anti-node'. Thus the string of harmonic loops is created. A supposed straight line between the loops going through the nodes is called 'equilibrium.' The point where one medium ends and another medium starts is defined as the 'boundary' and the behaviour of the wave at the end of a medium is referred to as the 'boundary behaviour.' The boundary behaviours are categorized as the fixed end reflection, free end reflection, and the transmission of pulse at the boundary from less dense medium to a denser medium, or the transmission from denser medium to a less dense medium.[11] All kinds of waves, including water and light, have the quality of having reflection, refraction or diffraction.

Energy flow in bio signalling is achieved with the combined action of positively charged protons (+1) and negatively charged electrons (-1), and the neutrons (0) to balance them. Energy flow in waves is achieved with the combined interaction of the 'positron,' also called anti-electron or positive 'electron' that has positive charge and the electron has negative charge and all are balanced with the 'neutrino' that has neutral charge, which is from the family of neutral leptons.

The energy of photon "light" depends on the radiation frequency; there are photons of all energies from high-energy gamma and x-rays, through visible light, to low energy infrared and radio waves. All photons travel at the speed of light. Considered among subatomic particles, photons are bosons, having no electric charge or rest mass (zero) and 1/2 unit of spin; they are field particles that are thought to be the carriers of the electromagnetic field.[12]

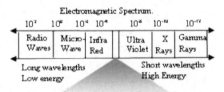
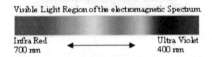

Image 6: Visible and invisible light waves. © 2014, Shukran Publishing. Used with permission

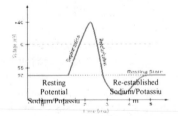

Image 7: Action Potential. © 2014, Shukran Publishing. Used with permission

Energy force in the action potential generates the level and strength of the communication between the brain and body, determining the end behaviour. Value of an intake at first instant will determine the level of chemicals (neurotransmitters) released into the system. Thus, the behaviour of the beginning will determine the behaviour of the whole neurobiological system and the end result of the behaviour. It will carry on and on until the behaviour of the free-willed input is changed, then the output will be changed accordingly. This is the only place where the freedom of choice in determining energy behaviour is involved.

In proportion, comparing the free will to the rest of the automated system, it is almost next to nothing, however, it is a fundamental vital point that it can determine the behaviour of the whole system to a certain level. It does not only affect its own biological, psychological, spiritual body, soul and spirit but also related actions can affect the other social interrelations. Therefore, we need to know the relationships of the first firing impact, which takes place in the cell

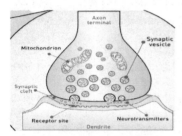

Image 8: Synapses.
© 2014, Shukran Publishing.
Used with permission

bodies, in the brain, and the strength level of the neurotransmitters released into the synaptic gaps (cleft), and the capacity of the target cells whether they are able to take it in or not.

Neuron, once it is triggered by a stimulus of the negative electrical potential force, becomes positive and begins to produce waves of impulses, then, the depolarizing receptor potential spreads down the sensory neuron until it reaches a specialized portion of membrane called the triggered zone; at the triggered zone the receptor potential is converted into action potentials, the number and the frequency of the action potentials is directly related to the amplitude and duration of the receptor potential - and the amount of neurotransmitter released at the axon terminals of the sensory neuron is a function of the number and frequency of action potentials generated.

> Some neurons such as those that release the neurotransmitters dopamine or serotonin (neurotransmitters that effect mood, arousal and our sense of well being) fire action potentials spontaneously and continuously (1 to 20 times per second), producing a steady stream (tonic release) of neurotransmitter. Other neurons... require the action of excitatory synaptic inputs in order to bring them to their firing threshold.[13]

Neurons in the peripheral autonomic nervous system have repetitive firing rates that are called 'inhibitory neurons.' They have impulses in steady stream waves and they are usually placed in the brain and in the spinal cord. Neurons that are in the peripheral somatic nervous system need stimuli to reach the firing threshold rate. They are called 'excitatory neurons.' The level of the stimuli, voluntarily controlled, will determine the level of strength, speed and force of the wave impulses in the action potential. However, the 'proper dynamics in neuronal

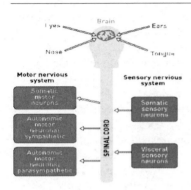

Image 9: Nervous System.
© 2014, Shukran Publishing.
Used with permission

network can only be maintained if the excitatory forces are counteracted by the effective inhibitory forces.'[14]

Unity, in acting together between the two nervous systems, is as vital as in the other areas of existence. Every single part of the body needs to be working in a free, equal and just manner without oppressing each other. They do not interrupt the work of the others, are not interrupted by the others and have no resistance to working in cooperation, as it should be. However, in the case of an emergency, certain vital points are fused with extra sensitive and flexible systems. For example, the 'pyramidal neurons' in the forebrain structure and the 'Sino Atrial Node'

(SAN) in the heart structure work as the 'potential pacemakers' within the body. There are, in abundance, different types of pyramidal neurons found in the forebrain structures but not in the other parts of the brain, striatum, midbrain and hindbrain or in the spinal cord. They are excitatory cells that play important roles in circuiting, integrating, polarizing and depolarizing incoming excitatory and inhibitory signals. They sort and send the signals to all related and associated target compartments within the brain and outside.

Thus, the power of input is directed and diverted to many different related points that give time for the system to divert and balance the power of the input, saving itself from a sudden potentially threatening impact.

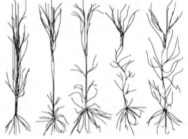

CA3   Layer V   Layer III   Cubiculum   CA1

Image 10: Examples of the Pyramidal neurons.
© 2014, Shukran Publishing.
Used with permission

In addition to being influenced by the strength and spatial location of the activated synapses, dendritic integration is influenced by voltage-gated ion channels, which are abundant in pyramidal neuron dendrites (Johnston et al.1996). The voltage-gated $Na+$, $Ca2+$, $K+$ channels in pyramidal neurons dendrites make the dendrites excitable, which means they are capable of

> nonlinear integration that includes a variety of types of dendritic action potentials... Other types of voltage-gated channels... include A- type K+ channels and hyperpolarisation-activated caption channels, (also known as HCN channels).[15]

Scientists state that there are around a hundred different types of chemicals released through neurotransmitters within the both, 'CNS and PNS' nervous systems. The most important chemicals are: dopamine (DA or DOPA); serotonin; acetylcholine (ACh); noradrenaline; glutamate; endorphin and enkephalin. The types, amount and the speed of the released chemicals depend on the information input collectively from the sensory organs and conscious mind, assisted or hindered by individual genetically characterized ability and aided by the inhibitory motor neurons if they are not physically disabled.

Low levels of dopamine in the body lead to Parkinson's disease and high levels of it to schizophrenia and hallucinations. Serotonin, (5-hydoxytryptamine, 5-HT) is known as 'the feel-good' chemical, and low levels can cause severe or mild depression, panic and fear depending on the level. High level can cause artificial tranquillity and optimism, which can create a risk of not being able to estimate danger. 'Acetylcholine is critical for communication between neurons and muscle at the neuromuscular junction, is involved in direct neurotransmission in autonomic ganglia, and has been implicated in cognitive processing, arousal, and attention in the brain.'[16]

Deficiency of acetylcholine in the brain affects memory and in severe cases it can cause Alzheimer's disease. Outside the brain, it activates and regulates muscle movements such as heart rates, digestion, secretion of saliva, and bladder function. The chemical called noradrenaline is produced in the 'lucus coeruleus,' which is a part of the brain that is called the brain's pleasure centre.

> The activation of locus coeruleus neurons provides a central command that increases noradrenaline release in its multiple target regions, although noradrenaline release by locus coeruleus terminals is also controlled by local mechanisms. Noradrenaline has complex neuromodulatory effects on neuronal activity and it is essential for several cognitive functions.[17]

It also regulates the reflex of 'fight or flight' response. Accordingly, it involves the heart rate, blood pressure and gastrointestinal functions as well. Thus, an unbalanced transmission will affect all of the related parts of the body owing to the miraculously calculated dose of interference to create the exact balance needed by the body.

The other chemical, glutamate, 'is the most prevalent excitatory neurotransmitter in the mammalian CNS'[18] and involves most aspects of normal brain functioning including cognition, memory and learning. The precise level and the time of the neurotransmission of glutamate are very important. High-level glutamate in the system, usually taken in through fast food or other means, can create a toxin called 'glutamate excitotoxicity.' This alters the natural balance between the neurotransmitter release and the receptor, and the accumulated glutamate in the connection area kills the surrounding neurons.

Endorphin and enkephalin, the major chemicals, are also known as the natural painkillers of the body.

> There is thought to be a link between stress, the body's natural painkillers and the immune system. In 1975, it was discovered that the body makes its own natural painkillers, morphine-like substances called endorphins and enkephalins…Endorphins are found in the pituitary gland and, although their exact role in stress reaction is still unclear, several studies have suggested that they may help to mediate the body's response to stressful stimuli.[19]

Enkephalins can be produced through meditation and by some other kinds of activities.

> The human body produces at least 20 different endorphins with possible benefits and uses that researchers are investigating. Beta-endorphin appears to be the endorphin that seems to have the strongest effect on the brain and body during exercise. Endorphins are believed to produce four key effects on body and mind: they enhance the immune system, they relieve pain, and they reduce stress, and postpone the aging process…Recent studies have found that nutritional and biochemical imbalances, rather than lack of will power or character, may increase the potential for substance abuse. Specifically, alcohol and drugs give temporary relief for a depleted endorphin level, which is one reason why they produce addiction.[20]

Endorphin sounds very good for the health when it is naturally produced but, receiving too much too soon can also cause problems in coping with everyday life requirements.

Heart is the pumping centre of the circulatory system. Even though all the cardiac cells are automated, the heart's working system is influenced and affected by emotions through the level of the synaptic messages.

The beating heart ensures that every cell of the body has an uninterrupted supply of food, oxygen, and other essentials. So powerful is it that the heart can pump the body's entire blood volume of 5 litres (8.8 pints) around the body about every minute. On average it beats, or pumps 70 times a minute when the body is at rest, yet can increase this rate if the body is more active. Over a life time of 70 years, the heart beats some 2.5 billion times without tiring or stopping for a rest...[21]

Heartbeat works in a cycle, and the entire cycle is initiated from the 'Sino Atrial' (SA) node, which is the natural pacemaker of the heart's beat as mentioned above. The heartbeat cycle has its own electrical pathways within itself, independent of every other part. Electric pulse is initiated from the SA node and received by the Atria Ventricular (AV) node, which is 'a small bundle of specialized cells located at the junction of the atria and ventricles. It is the only point where an action potential originating at SA node can spread to the ventricles.'[22]

There are two pathways going out from the SA node, the 'interatrial pathway' and the 'internodal pathway.' The interatrial pathway goes from the SA node to the left atrium ensuring the depolarization of the cycle. The internodal pathway is the action potential connection between the SA node and the VA node that sends the signals to a bundle of nerves, which are called 'the bundle of His,' after a brief delay to give time for depolarization. 'His bundle' then send the action potential down the interventricular septum, to the nerves that are called 'the Purkinje fibbers,' which are extended from the bundle of His. Finally, the action potential sent from the SA node goes through the AV node to the bottom part of the heart and the action potential is repolarised throughout the ventricular myocardium and is ready for the next cycle.

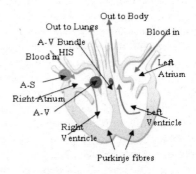

Image 11: Heart Structure.
© 2014, Shukran Publishing.
Used with permission.

It is amazing to see how every single cell is kept alive by the circulation of the blood pumped by the heart carrying to them nutrients and oxygen and taking away from them waste materials and carbon dioxide. It is obvious that any slight imbalance in the system can cause many types of problems according to its seriousness. Heart does not only regulate blood in the physical body but also seems regulate the unseen emotional feelings. We never refer to 'broken mind or brain' but we do have sayings of broken heart, as well as loving or hating from the heart, telling, feeling from the heart etc. We have a certain level of control in our minds but the heart can overpower and can control us. Therefore, it is the strongest and the most vulnerable part of the body, affected by emotions as well as mishandling of the physical systems. In 2007 American Heart and American Stroke Associations estimated 700,000 Americans would have a new coronary attack and about 500,000 would have a recurrent attack. 'It is estimated that an additional 175,000 silent first heart attacks occur each year.'[23] So, there must be something drastically wrong in the handling of the heart. Could it be the absence of the instruction manual of the codes and coordinates to see how one could unite the voluntary actions with the automated ones to coordinate them correctly, which will let the heart be free from every kind of oppression from self and others to work in peaceful harmony within and without.

Every cell in the body has its own special working order to accomplish its own duty as well as cooperating, giving and taking, within the working order of self and the surrounding cells to accomplish harmony. This clearly resembles every individual being like a cell in the body of humanity. Every individual system in the body, like brain and heart, has its own individual working order in harmony within self and unity with the others. As long as they are not damaged or distorted in one way or another, they work perfectly in an automated manner. The important point here is that they all need energy impulses to stream through from initiation point to the target, polarizing and depolarizing. They also have pressure points in case of emergency to absorb or back up in extraordinary situations and have fuse points, diverting and spreading the power received in a wider area in case of a sudden shock.

What about the parts working under human free will, which may be too little in proportion but too powerful in effect? Have they the force to overpower the automated system, and if yes, how? This point alone proves that human beings are in need of authentic codes and coordinations for establishing valid links within the body itself to work in harmony. However, freedom, equality and justice cannot ever be established correctly without the knowledge (revelations) from a higher intellect, the same authority that has the power and knowledge above any created power and knowledge, including the voluntary actions. The planner and producer of all systems, the Creator, is called the Deity when instructing His creations how to act and He is called the Lord when He takes the full responsibility for looking after them while the system is working. Even though He knows the best for them in an absolute independent manner, He hands over a little portion of it to human free will.

Therefore, the meanings of Deity and the Lord are interwoven together, the Originator, the Creator, the Manager and the Caretaker, all in the One. Therefore, unity in the system can only be accomplished if it is managed by the same unified source of authority. None the less, human beings can only achieve the unity within self and others if they willingly choose to follow the fundamental instructions of the same source for their basic voluntary actions. Only then, can they have the correct pin codes for their actions to join the rest. After establishing the essential foundation, human beings can develop the required individual, social and environmental details according to their own needs, whatever, whenever and wherever they are. Otherwise, it is impossible to know or guess the coordinations of such a complicated system to unify within self, with others, let alone with the Creator, as the Deity.

Historical evidence indicates that human beings always had some kind of awareness about the existence of the Super Power behind all creation. However, they still tend to choose a deity or deities voluntarily other then the Creator unlike the rest of creation. Therefore, while the idea of the existence of a unique Creator remained constant, deified objects or people kept changing according to the necessities of the time and place in which human beings lived. Even certain objects, such as the sun, the earth, eagles, goats, or people as leaders were idolized, either voluntarily or at times by force. Nonetheless, they submitted themselves fully to the service of their chosen or imposed deity or deities while regulating their individual and social everyday life orders according to the values of the chosen deity or deities. Hammurabi, (1792-1750 BC)[24] was the king of Babylon who laid down the first written social rules and regulations but we have no evidence that he was taken as a deity. However, there is plenty of evidence indicating that Pharaohs openly declared themselves as deities, using their authority to be obeyed fully. They ruled people under their unauthenticated knowledge and unjust authority for a long period of time, 3100 BC to 332 BC.[25]

The meaning of deity becomes more visible in mythology with the concept of fantasized invisible deities. Cosmological self-imagined deity stories were used as the source of knowledge and authority to identify the self and customize cultures. Consequently, people, matters, objects, animals, myths, magic, dreams, certain ornaments and the products of human imagination became a deity or deities. Minds, cultural identities and life patterns were shaped, ruled and regulated under the name of these deities, when in fact, they were the products of the thoughts and imaginations of human beings themselves. These kinds of unauthentic and unauthorized attempts for establishing interrelations between the conscious voluntary actions and the pre-programmed actions are not only bound to destroy freedom, equality and justice between them but also damage both systems by leaving the doors wide open for oppression, anger, division, chaos, fear and anxiety to flourish.

Philosophy, on the other hand, places the human rational intellect right in the centre and demanded that it should think, know, decide and act for its own sake alone. Yet again, it is idolizing its own self-devised personal rules and regulations. This gave individuals a chance to think and decide for themselves, which was very much lacking at the time. But the necessity for authentic knowledge was totally ignored, which was essential for a valid relationship between the human voluntary actions and the built-in automated intellects. In the meantime, the appearance of so many different speculative philosophical approaches and the methods such as realism, idealism, mysticism and scepticism and so on were tearing people into pieces.[26]

We now know that an unauthenticated conscious intellect alone, no matter how wise, can not meet the authentic need of the whole existence to have a peaceful and perfect integration between the human body, soul and voluntary actions of every individual, let alone between cultures, societies or the Creator as the Deity. For example, Diogenes Laertius (400-325 BC). who consciously decided to give up reasoning altogether and lived like an animal on the street. or Pyrrho of Elis (365-275 BC) on the other hand, who searched for reason alone in everything.[27] In these cases, the outcome would always be biased, which would create fear and anxiety that is simply due to the unjust oppression of an unauthentic authority, either on the self or on the others.

Revelations, on the other hand, share the same message about choosing the authentic deity and let individuals free to choose. Hence, the first commandment in the Ten Commandments states that 'I am the Lord (Rab) your God (Creator) who brought you out of Egypt, out of land of slavery. You shall have no other gods (deities) before Me.'[28]

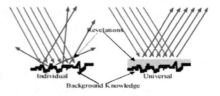

Image 12: Diffuse and Specular Reflections of revealed Knowledge. © 2014, Shukran Publishing. Used with permission.

The New Testament declares the same, 'Jesus said to him, "Away from me, Satan! For it is written: 'Worship the Lord your God (Deity), and serve him only".'[29]

And The Qur'an says, 'Your deity is one only, there is no other deity (Ilah) but Allah, Who has the immeasurable mercy for the entire and the special.'[30] Revelations with the same messages aim to establish the essential foundation for developing authentic and scientific knowledge to meet individual and universal needs for interacting with each other in the most perfect harmony.

All the revelations emphasise the importance of the authenticated knowledge, either coming from the scientific resources or the Creator, to establish a universally valid base for all human kinds to stand on firmly first. They will be free, equal and just in order to be able to take individual and collective voluntarily chosen actions while interacting with self, others and with the deity. The revelations aim to provide valid information to satisfy the uneven surface of individuality, on one hand, and to unite the basics of cultural and universal differences on the other. They also intend to hold basic authentic keys for codes, coordination and the necessary practical skills for combining and correlating the actions of both pre-programmed and conscious human voluntary intellects. When the knowledge of revelations from the Creator as the Higher Intellect is authenticated by science, then the maximum harmony and the minimum fear and anxiety would be achieved between the entire pre-programmed and voluntary energy networks.

Whether the human race came down from Heaven and spread from one mother and father or evolved from another human-like creature, they are in fact units of equals with similar strengths and weaknesses that only slightly vary according to genetic, physical, cultural, religious and environmental backgrounds. In fact, some of these differences are almost disappearing with the development of the Internet network in the twenty-first century. Whether this kind of network can be considered to be taking place of a deity or not yet needs to be studied. Nonetheless, this ultrafast and vast change in the world's life style is mesmerizing people more than ever before. At the moment, it is in its chaos stage like it was at the beginning of the universe. While the gaps in unknowns, about self and others are closing on one side, but the further unknown gaps are created on the other. Such assimilated but practically not yet understood information can cause excessive disturbance in human perception that is naturally reflected on every aspect of life.

While life journeys towards an unknown fixed destination, it also revolves around itself at the same time. This system is similar to the voluntary choice of deity. A fixed aim is necessary to have a secured lifeline equilibrium to follow during the unsteady emotional journey of life. Happiness, sadness, hope and fear are the basic driving forces behind the aims and objectives that involve every aspect of physical, psychological, bio-psychological and social life.

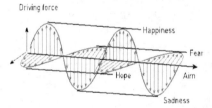

Image 13: Basic Emotion Waves.
© 2014, Shukran Publishing.
Used with permission.

Equal or non-equal, if any creation or creations with similar nature are selected as a deity or deities, it will cause serious destruction in the frequency of the energy network flow. This will result in psychological, biological and social disturbance between the chosen deity, the chooser and the surroundings. They are all creations themselves and cannot be the genuine sources of happiness and sadness or hope and fear to fully satisfy the individual and the universal human needs. Besides, any uneasiness of feelings of indebtedness, desire for revenge, expecting favour, or fear from creations alike will put the energy flow between them under a tremendous pressure. To be able to understand this better we can now look into the involuntary energy wave end behaviours when they meet different mediums. The same laws apply within the human body and mind, the only thing is that some voluntary and involuntary actions are interwoven and the action potentials are triggered by free will that could affect the whole body, soul, spirit and the end behaviour as explained above. Therefore, the right choice of target and actions is necessary for the released energy waves to have balanced construction and positive end result for the well being of self and others.

When the actual authentic source is selected as the deity, there will be no disturbance in the network of energy flow, back and forth. Authenticated adequate amount of incoming and outgoing energy flow will strengthen the choosers to the maximum level possible. Then, there will be no energy distortion diversion or clashes that will take place between the pre-programmed and conscious voluntary actions. Now, we can look into the existing four types of 'energy wave end boundary behaviours,' which scientifically explain these energy-transferring interrelations very well.[31]

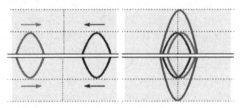

Image 14: Positive and Negative Wave Interferences before and during.
© 2014, Shukran Publishing.
Used with permission

There is no human being who exists without a deity or deities to turn to, for thanking or seeking help to satisfy their own emotions like happiness, sadness, hope and fear. However, an unguarded sudden incoming energy shock can take place in every one, even in strong believers, which is compared here with the 'free wave end boundary behaviour.' Both 'constructive' (+) and 'destructive' (-) waves in the free end boundary behaviour can become the most destructive waves on the nervous system.

Once an unguarded positive 'happiness' or negative 'sadness' input energy signal enters through the senses, it reflects back with double strength, the higher the value of input, the stronger the reflected value will be. '...The restoring force (power that works against the wave) is zero and the reflected (soft) wave has the same polarity...'[32]

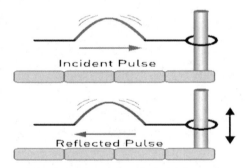

Image 15: Free end Wave Behaviour.
© 2014, Shukran Publishing.
Used with permission.

When a reflected pulse meets with the incoming incident pulse from the opposite direction on the same side of the medium, both values will be added up together but as soon as the waves pass each other, each will carry their own original value, and the sequence will carry on until the waves reach their targets. If the reflected pulse hits the target when it is in its highest point on the same

medium, joined with released incident pulse, it can distort or jam the system altogether depending on the level of their combined strength.

Therefore, waves intensified on the same side of the same medium are more likely to cause serious psychological and biological damage, becoming lethal at times. For example, Eymen, a Syrian girl running from the war in 2013, met a Turkish boy; they fell in love and got married. Two months later her brother, whom she had not seen for a long time, came from Syria and wanted to surprise his sister, telling everyone not to let her know about his coming. Unfortunately, Eymen's nervous system could not cope with so much happiness at once and she died there and then from a sudden shock when she saw her brother unexpectedly.[33]

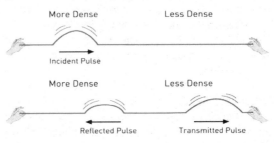

Image 16: A wave Travelling from a More Dense to a Less Dense Medium. © 2014, Shukran Publishing. Used with permission.

Unlike the free wave end boundary behaviour, some power transmission can take place between the two different mediums, depending on the ratio of the density difference in between. In the case of choosing a deity that has a 'less dense medium' than human nature, the transmitted pulse will carry some values of the incident pulse away but it will have some values left behind to return back. The value of both pulses will depend on the ratio difference between the mediums.

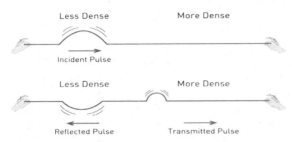

Image 17: A wave travelling from a Less dense to a More Dense Medium. © 2014, Shukran Publishing. Used with permission.

Positive or negative, the reflected pulse will behave the same. The value of incident and reflected pulses will add up when they meet, but carry on with the same value of their own after passing through each other. Therefore, returning value (+,-) will always be more than the value of the first released incident pulse.

In the case of choosing a deity that has a 'denser

medium' than human nature it works in a similar way, apart from the position of the reflected pulse and the behaviour. The reflected pulse becomes an inverted reflected pulse after transmitting some of its value to the next denser medium yet again, depending on their density ratio difference. This time, due to the behaviour of inverted reflected pulse, the value of the higher pulse will be reduced by the amount of the lower pulse when both pulses meet on the same medium but they will carry on their own original values after passing through each other. This will reduce the value of the incident pulse according to the value of the reflected pulse but it will never be fully neutralized. In both cases, whatever and whoever the chosen deity might be, there will be some power transmitted and some returned back, adding on to the first released incident pulse, which will never allow total neutralization.

This means that valid communication codes between pre-programmed and conscious voluntary systems have not been completely achieved. The amount of interaction that takes place demonstrates the ability and the level of sharing work between the existing programmes. Unbalanced wave transmissions, either low or high, cannot assist the nervous system in a correct manner, especially synapses, to work in the most possible harmonic manner. In both cases, lower or higher energy flow, problems will arise and damage the human biology and biopsychology slowly and steadily in the long term.[34]

The chosen deity and the chooser must both have fully validated capacities for the 'fixed end boundary behaviour' to take place. In our case, on one end, there is the Creator that no energy waves can go beyond, as He is the actual source of all kinds of energy waves and on the other end is the human heart that has the ability to go beyond all kind of reasoning. But, this is still a matter of debate, some scholars think that it is the 'mind'[35] as it is the first place that energy waves are triggered but more incline towards the 'heart.'[36] The heart is capable of believing in the Creating power even without seeing, hearing, touching or having any figure in mind, which is one of the distinct qualities of being the Deity. It not only, has the ability to receive and redirect the received energy signals to the actual source directly, but also has the ability to narrow it down, channelling it to the node connection, which can take place on the same equilibrium of the same medium so that time and space can disappear, alongside with fear and anxiety. The heart also has the ability to receive and reflect the secondary energy input coming through the

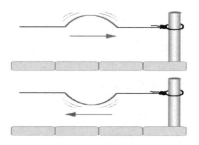

Image 18: Fixed end Wave Boundary Behaviour.
© 2014, Shukran Publishing.
Used with permission.

senses depending on the individual varied level of knowledge, reasoning and believing.

Unlike the other wave end behaviours, the total balance of neutralization in the same medium can take

place only with fixed end boundary behaviour: '...Since the end is clamped, it cannot move...According to Newton's third law, the wall (end) must be exerting an equal download force on the end of string. This new force creates a wave pulse that propagates from right to left with the same speed of the incident wave, but in opposite polarity... at the fixed (hard) boundary, the displacement remains zero...'[37]

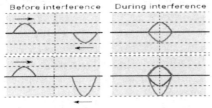

Image19: Positive and Negative Wave Interferences of Fixed End Boundary Behaviour.
© 2014, Shukran Publishing. Used with permission.

The power of the reflected inverted wave stays at the same value of the incident wave but of an opposite value. It is the same for negative and positive waves. When the both pulses (+, -) with the same value meet on the same medium they can totally neutralize each other resting on the equilibrium, where time and space disappear. When one of the pulses, incident or reflective, has higher and the other has lower value, the higher one will be reduced by the value of the lower one when they meet but carry on with their own values after passing through. In any case, the value of the reflected pulse will always have lesser value than the incident pulse fist released. Therefore, it has the ability to neutralize and balance the waves and the wave end behaviours to the best beneficial manner that reflects on to the body, soul, spirit and the social relations.

Therefore, choosing the actual energy source as the only Deity, facilitates all, pre-programmed, emotional and conscious voluntary actions to work together in best possible harmony. When the total neutralization is achieved between the two fixed ends on the same equilibrium the unification of the source and the receiver can take place. Unfortunately, '...human beings are 'by nature equal' in both body and intellect bur are tragically distorted by our first-person perspective...'[38] For this reason, to achieve a hundred per cent correlation between them is almost impossible. Besides, a deity, either chosen from within self, such as ego, knowledge, strength of power or from outside the self, such as position, wealth, family heritage, or any thing made of matter or imagination, is always a created being. They may have various energy levels, lower or higher but will never meet the every individual human need fully, as all the creations are dependent on each other, nourished by the same energy source, and governed by the same higher

intellect. They can have certain levels of interaction abilities between them but none is independent of the other to have total authority over one another.

Indeed, fixed end wave boundary behaviour demonstrates that human voluntary actions involving psychology, biology and sociology have no other options but to join the rest of the creations by choosing the Creator as the Deity in order to attain harmonised integration using the valid codes and coordinations. In fact, the higher the level of freedom, equality and justice achieved among these interrelations, the better the level of happiness, health and social relations will be. Therefore, human beings need to do sincere and serious researches to find out about these authentic bases to act upon during the voluntary free willed actions, which are pre-set for the others. So, new research is vital to explore existing energy network behaviours so that we may differentiate the right connections from the wrong between the human body, soul and spirit, individual humans and other beings, and the chosen deity. This research needs to be done under totally new individual and universal objective approaches, using totally new scientific methods to meet the demand of human needs in the twenty-first century and beyond.

No doubt that there are more questions waiting to be answered. For example, 'Why do none of the other existing beings coming through the Big Bang have any conscious voluntary intellects to choose their own actions and deity such as human beings have?' 'Is it possible that human beings have another link to the Creator apart from the Big Bang?' 'Is it possible to unite both, the Creator and the human heart as conscious receivers, to interact together without time and space being involved?' The latest progress in these fields seems to indicate that human beings, still need to search for many more centuries to come, to be able to answer these questions.

Notes

[1] John D. Barrow, *The Origin of the Universe* (London: The Orion Publishing Group, 1994), 10.
[2] Brian Greene, *The Elegant Universe* (London: Vintage Press, 2000), 82, 346.
[3] Thomas Crump, *A Brief History of Science* (London: Constable & Robinson Ltd. Press, 2002), 120-126.
[4] Neil F. Comins, Thomas Krause and William J. Kaufmann, *Discovering the Universe* (NY: Freeman, W. H. & Company Press, 2003), 104.
[5] Ibid.
[6] Thomas Crump, *A Brief History of Science: As Seen through the Development of Scientific Instruments* (London: Constable & Robinson Ltd. Publishers, 2002), 229.
[7] Comins, Krause and Kaufmann, *Discovering The Universe*, 106.
[8] Ibid., 106.
[9] Ibid., 435-36.

[10] Ibid., 438.

[11] Sukran Karatas, *Deity and Freedom, Equality, Justice in History, Philosophy, Science Deity and Freedom* (Turkey: Shukran Publishing Press, 2013), 339-350.

[12] 'Photon' and 'Subatomic Particle,' in *EncyclopediaBritannica*.com, viewed on 31 January 2015, http://www.britannica.com/EBchecked/topic/458038/photon.

[13] Open University Course Team, *From Cells to Consciousness* (Milton Keynes: Open University Press, 2007), 28-29.

[14] Peter Jonas and Gyorgy Buzsaki, 'Neural Inhibition,' *Scholarpedia* website, viewed on 31 January 2015, http://www.scholarpedia.org/article/Neural_inhibition.

[15] Andreas Frick, Jeffrey Magee and Daniel Johnston, 'LTP is Accompanied by an Enhanced Local Excitability of Pyramidal Neuron Dendrites,' *Nature Neuroscience* 2 (2004): 1, abstract viewed on 31 January 2015, http://www.ncbi.nlm.nih.gov/pubmed/14730307.

[16] Marina R. Picciotto, Meenakshi Alreja and J. David Jentsch, 'Acetylcholine,' in N*europsychopharmacology: The Fifth Generation of Progress*, ed. Kanneth L. Davis, et al. (Philadelphia: American College of Neuropsychopharmacology, 2002), 11.

[17] Sebastien Bouret and Susan J. Sara, 'Locus Coeruleus,' *Scholarpedia* website, viewed on 31 January 2015, http://www.scholarpedia.org/article/Locus_coeruleus.

[18] John P. J. Pinel, *Biopsychology* (USA: Allyn and Bacon Press, 1990), 114.

[19] Richard Gross, *Psychology: The Science of Mind and Behaviour* (London: Hodder and Stoughton, 1996), 145.

[20] Bonnie O'Sullivan, 'What are Endorphins?' viewed on 31 January 2015, http://www.road-to-health.com/64/What_are_Endorphins_.html.

[21] S. Ranjan, 'Genoderma and Heart,' viewed on 31 January 2015, http://www.dxnmalaysia.com/healthinfo/gano_heart.php.

[22] 'AV Node and Bundle of His,' viewed on 31 January 2015, http://zaf.biol.pmf.unizg.hr/anphys/provodjenje%20impulsa.html.

[23] American Heart and American Stroke Associations, 'Heart Disease and Stroke Statistics,' viewed on 31 January 2015, http://www.harcdata.org/UserFiles/File/AHA-heartandstrokestats.pdf.

[24] Robert A. Guisepi and F. Roy Williams, 'The Akkadians,' *World History Project* website, viewed on 1 March 2013, http://history-world.org/sargon_the_great.htm.

[25] Wim van den Dugen, 'King Unas Corridors, West Wall (313-317) and East Wall (230-319),' viewed on 1 March 2013, http://maat.sofiatopia.org/wenis13.htm.

[26] Wilhelm Windelband, *A History of Philosophy*, trans. James H. Tufts (New York: Elibron Classics by Adamant Media Corporation Press, 2006), 328-337.

[27] Bertrand Russell, *History of Western Philosophy* (London: Routledge Press, 1993), 240, 42, 43.

[28] *The Holy Bible, New International Version* (London: British Library Publication, 1987), Ex 20:1.

[29] Ibid., Mt 4:10.

[30] Abdullah Yusuf Ali, *The Holy Qur'an* (USA: Amana Group Press, 1983), Bakara 2:163.

[31] Karatas, *Deity and Freedom*, 344-348.

[32] Daniel A. Russell, 'Reflection of Waves from Boundaries,' viewed on 31 January 2015, http://www.acs.psu.edu/drussell/Demos/reflect/reflect.html.

[33] 'Surprise Visit Brought Death,' *Milliyet.com.tr* website, posted 24 December 2013, viewed December 2013, viewed on 31 January 2015, http://www.milliyet.com.tr/surpriz-ziyaret-olum%20getirdi/gundem/detay/1812317/default.htm?ShowPageSkin=1.

[34] Karatas, *Deity and Freedom*, 377-379.

[35] Bertrand Russell, *History of Western Philosophy*, 151.

[36] William Montgomery Watt, *The Faith and Practice of Al-Ghazali* (Oxford: Oneworld Publishers Online Press, 1994), 74, viewed on 24 December 2013, http://www.persica.net/stamford/GhazaliDeliveranceFromError.pdf.

[37] Russell, 'Reflection of Waves from Boundaries.'

[38] Daniel M. Gross, *The Secret History of Emotions: From Aristotle's Rhetoric to Modern Brain Science* (London: The University of Chicago Press, 2006), 45.

Bibliography

Barrow, John D. *The Origin of the Universe*. London: The Orion Publishing Group, 1994.

Comins, Neil F., Thomas Krause, and William J. Kaufmann. *Discovering the Universe*. Publisher: Freeman, W. H. & Company Press, 2003.

Crump, Thomas. *A Brief History of Science: As Seen through the Development of Scientific Instruments*. London: Constable & Robinson Ltd. Publishers, 2002.

Frick, Andreas, Jeffrey Magee, and Daniel Johnston. 'LTP is Accompanied by an Enhanced Local Excitability of Pyramidal Neuron Dendrites.' *Nature Neuroscience* 2 (2004): 126-35.

Greene, Brian. *The Elegant Universe*. London: Vintage Publishers, 2000.

Gross, Daniel M. *The Secret History of Emotions: From Aristotle's Rhetoric to Modern Brain Science*. London: The University of Chicago Press, 2006.

Gross, Richard. *Psychology: The Science of Mind and Behaviour*. London: Hodder and Stoughton, 1996.

Karatas, Sukran. *Deity and Freedom, Equality, Justice in History, Philosophy, Science*. Turkey: Shukran Publishing Press, 2013.

Open University Course Team. *From Cells to Consciousness*. Milton Keynes: Open University Press, 2007.

Picciotto, Marina R., Meenakshi Alreja, and J. David Jentsch. 'Acetylcholine.' In *Neuropsychopharmacology: The Fifth Generation of Progress*, edited by Kenneth L. Davis, Dennis Charney, Joseph T. Coyle, and Charles Nemeroff, 3-14. Philadelphia, Pennsylvania: American College of Neuropsychopharmacology, 2002.

Pinel, John P.J. *Biopsychology*. USA: Allyn and Bacon Press, 1990.

Russell, Bertrand. *History of Western Philosophy*. London: Routledge Publication Press, 1993.

Watt, William Montgomery. *The Faith and Practice of Al-Ghazali*. Oxford: Oneworld Publishers Online Press, 1994.

Windelband, Wilhelm. *A History of Philosophy*. Translated by James H. Tufts. New York: Elibron Classics, Adamant Media Corporation Press, 2006.

Websites:

American Heart and American Stroke Associations. 'Heart Disease and Stroke Statistics.' Viewed on 31 January 2015. http://www.harcdata.org/UserFiles/File/AHA-heartandstrokestats.pdf.

'AV Node and Bundle of His.' Viewed on 31 January 2015. http://zaf.biol.pmf.unizg.hr/anphys/provodjenje%20impulsa.html.

Bouret, Sebastien, and Susan J. Sara. 'Locus Coeruleus.' *Scholarpedia* website. Viewed on 31 January 2015. http://www.scholarpedia.org/article/Locus_coeruleus.

Guisepi, Robert A., and F. Roy Williams. 'The Akkadians.' *World History Project* website. Viewed on 1 March 2013. http://history-world.org/sargon_the_great.htm.

Jonas, Peter, and Gyorgy Buzsaki. 'Neural inhibition,' *Scholarpedia* website. Viewed on 31 January 2015. http://www.scholarpedia.org/article/Neural_inhibition.

O'Sullivan, Bonnie. 'What are Endorphins?' Viewed on 31 January 2015. http://www.road-to-health.com/64/What_are_Endorphins_.html.

'Photon' and 'Subatomic Particle.' *Encyclopedia Britannica* website. Viewed on 31 January 2015. http://www.britannica.com/EBchecked/topic/458038/photon.

Ranjan S. 'Genoderma and Heart.' Viewed on 31 January 2015. http://www.dxnmalaysia.com/healthinfo/gano_heart.php.

Russell, Daniel A. 'Reflection of Waves from Boundaries.' Viewed on 31 January 2015. http://www.acs.psu.edu/drussell/Demos/reflect/reflect.html.

'Surprise Visit Brought Death.' Viewed 24 December 2013. http://www.milliyet.com.tr/surpriz-ziyaret-lum%20getirdi/gundem/detay/1812317/default.htm?ShowPageSkin=1.

van den Dugen, Wim. 'King Unas Corridors, West Wall (313-317) and East Wall (230-319).' Viewed on 1 March 2013. http://maat.sofiatopia.org/wenis13.htm.

Sukran Karatas is a social science freelance researcher. Her main interest is to combine faith and science together to bring knowledge alive for the benefit of human health and happiness. She has written a book called, *Deity and Freedom, Equality, Justice in History, Philosophy, Science.'* Sukran is determined to see to it that new scientific research methods and solutions are developed for social sciences in the future.